The Media and Communications Study Skills Student Guide

Doug Specht

University of Westminster Press
www.uwestminsterpress.co.uk

Published by
University of Westminster Press
115 New Cavendish Street
London W1W 6XH
www.uwestminsterpress.co.uk

First published 2019

Cover design: Diana Jarvis; images shutterstock.com
Printed and bound by CPI Group (UK) Ltd, Croydon, CR0 4YY
Print and digital versions typeset by Siliconchips Services Ltd.

ISBN (Paperback): 978-1-912656-56-1
ISBN (PDF): 978-1-912656-57-8
ISBN (EPUB): 978-1-912656-58-5
ISBN (Kindle): 978-1-912656-59-2

DOI: https://doi.org/10.16997/book42

The full text of this book has been peer-reviewed to ensure high academic
standards. For full review policies, see: http://www.uwestminsterpress.co.uk/
site/publish/

To read the free, open access version of this book
online, visit https://www.uwestminsterpress.
co.uk/site/books/10.16997/book42
or scan this QR code with your mobile device:

Contents

CHAPTER I

Introduction: studying for a Masters degree

If you've picked up this book, it probably means you are just starting a degree in Media and Communications or one of the many sub-disciplines in the field, be that Journalism, Public Relations, Media Management, or Media and Campaigning, to name just a few. Firstly, welcome to a hugely exciting field. There was a time when people looked at media studies as not being a proper subject (boo!), but those days are long gone. Media and Communications courses are becoming ever more in demand, and ever more demanding. From late night editing sessions, placements in industry, lectures on theory from the Frankfurt School to Marxism, to the ethics of digital technology, and practical sessions on campaigning, sound engineering, marketing, and more, these courses are perhaps some of the most intensive around. Studying Media and Communications is far more than watching films and reading newspapers, it is about research, critical thinking, understanding the industry and the economics of media. It is about understanding and learning about people, society, interactions and how the world works, and who it works for, and who are excluded. As Professor Philip Thickett, former head of Birmingham City University's School of Media has said, 'media gives the people a voice or the skill to actually change people's views or lives […] that is why media matters.'[1] And he isn't alone in thinking that media and communications is important, former Channel 4 chief executive Michael Jackson, Sunday Times editor John Witherow, and hundreds of others have started their careers on Media and Communications courses. And with the second highest employment rate in the UK, why shouldn't you want to also be part of this exciting and diverse field that seeks to break down the barriers of incomprehension and mistrust? In a world of fake news, spin and

---

[1] See Quin-Jarvis (2014) for other quote sources and wider discussion.

How to cite this book chapter:
Specht, D. 2019. *The Media And Communications Study Skills Student Guide*. Pp. 1–3. London: University of Westminster Press. DOI: https://doi.org/10.16997/book42.a.

populism, one group of media professors made the argument (in the words of the article's strapline) that the subject has not only come of age but had 'finally found its place in the zeitgeist'.[2] It is also a degree which, as its name suggests, is hugely sociable, with a focus on talking to other people, studying other people, writing about people, interviewing people, meeting people. There are people everywhere. So, it is also a great way to make connections and friends around the world, creating your own *global village* as Marshall McLuhan might have said.

Balancing all of these elements above, along with the exciting social life that a Media and Communications course affords can be difficult. You will need to maintain your studies, and focus, through a degree that is very challenging. Your insitution will also want you to be both intellectually stimulated and to experience the pressures that you will encounter when you take up jobs within the media. You are going to be learning a whole heap of new skills and practice throughout your studies, and for the most part that is what your course, lectures, seminars and workshops are for. But there are two other elements that are common to all Media and Communications courses, that perhaps your standard modules won't help you with quite as much. These are, according to Professor James Curran, co-director of Goldsmiths Media Research Centre, 'the ability to write really well, a skill that most people don't have but makes a lot of media students highly employable', and in the words of Philip Thickett, 'the unspoken [requirement] of being on a pressurized course that reflects what people face in the industry'. These two skills, writing, and time management, form the backbone of what this book is all about. And if you have started this book by reading this introduction then you are already on the right path to great Media and Communication study skills. Even better, perhaps you read the blurb on the back first, skimmed through the contents pages and then thought, 'yes I'm going to read this'. These are some of the kinds of reading and study tactics that will be discussed through this book. We are getting ahead of ourselves though. Why should you keep reading this book? How will it help you in your studies?

There are hundreds of books out there that say they will help you in your studies, and thousands of pieces of advice. These range from the reasonably sound, such as Alexandre Dumas' system of using colour coded paper for writing in different genres, to the outright dangerous – French novelist Honoré de Balzac would drink 50 cups of coffee a day, a habit he shared with Voltaire – and in some cases just plain bizarre, such as Victor Hugo's idea that it is better to write in the nude (perhaps we should steer clear of French novelists and their advice). How do you know which is the right advice or whose to follow? How do you know what will work for you or your course? All difficult questions, and ones

---

[2] See Brabazon, T. et al. (2019).

that students around the world ask, regardless of their experience – and many of your lecturers might be asking these questions too, but they'd never tell you that.

This book isn't seeking to make the author his millions (it's free to download after all), and unlike other study skills books this one is designed as a daily companion to keep in your bag, to use as a reference guide in class, while writing essays, to help you negotiate group work, to give presentations and to get everything you can out of your studies. The book itself is filled with useful tips, quick methods, and plenty of places to practise the skills discussed. We also have a range of downloadable supplementary templates to help you organized and plan your studies and writing. This isn't just a book to read, it is a book that we will write together.

The book really covers two main themes, the first being about writing, and the second being more about general skills that will help you to navigate all kinds of other assessments and teaching techniques. Both are illustrated with templates, cheat sheets, activities, advice and links to other resources that might help you in your work. All these tips and resources have been collected together from many years of teaching. The author has also struggled with many of these things, and had to learn them the hard way… I only wish someone had written this book for me before I started my degree.

Everything in academia follows very specific patterns and forms, these are often the same across spoken and written forms and it is possible to learn these patterns, or at least to be aware of them, to enable you to produce better work within the *templates* of academia. This book is designed to help you do the best in your studies by helping you with the two elements highlighted by Thickett and Curran – writing and time management. And, unlike the patterns and templates it contains, this book can be read in any order, and you can skip and jump around between topics, but I do recommend starting with chapter 2 … it will ensure you have time to read the rest of the book.

So, let's get going …

References

Brabazon, T. (2019) Is media studies about to go viral? (THE) Times Higher Education Available at: https://www.timeshighereducation.com/features/media-studies-about-go-viral? (last accessed October 2019).
Quin-Jarvis, E. (2014) Media Studies: It's not a 'mickey mouse' degree. The Guardian [Online] Available from: https://www.theguardian.com/education/mortarboard/2014/feb/03/why-study-media-studies-students

CHAPTER 2

Why we study and setting goals

You've arrived! You are back at university, now for a Masters in Media and Communications. It might have been some time since you last studied, or maybe you have followed directly on from an undergraduate degree, but the questions are the same, why are you here? Should you have come? And how will you survive? Have no fear! This chapter starts by exploring these very questions, before taking us on a whistle stop introduction to goal setting, time management and how to stave off procrastination.

Media and Communications is an exciting field, helping us to come to terms with many of the things that define what it is to be human. To understand how we communicate – from the earliest times, through to the internet and social media – is to understand the history of humanity. And as the world becomes ever more mediated, that is how it becomes increasingly defined and controlled through technology, the study of Media and Communications becomes ever more important. The world, too can sometimes seem overwhelming, with the politics of fear and fake news influencing the way we live. And with stories of the psychological damage caused by social media and the 24-hour news cycle invading our homes and pockets, it can push us to want to hide from the world, and to feel powerless. A Masters degree in Media Studies though is designed to question and challenge these thoughts, helping you to think about what we mean by 'the media' and to question how we might study it. There are lots of different ways we can approach this, we can examine Media as technology, as a way of making meaning, through theories of everyday life, or workplace, as something that brings pleasure, or even as a destructive force. During your studies you might examine media production and organisation, analysis of media output, consumption, or even to ask bigger questions about the issue of media in society. These are approaches that will also be explored through a wide range of long standing debates and theories including 'political economy',

How to cite this book chapter:
Specht, D. 2019. *The Media And Communications Study Skills Student Guide*. Pp. 5–19.
London: University of Westminster Press. DOI: https://doi.org/10.16997/book42.b.
License: CC-BY-NC-ND 4.0

'critical race studies', 'psychoanalysis', 'feminist media theory', and these you will have to apply to all kinds of mediums, including radio, TV, cinema, internet, newspaper, advertising, and music). Throughout all of this, you will need to consider the way in which Media and Communications both reflect on, and shape and change the world around us. Given the range and complexity of (often) new ideas you will be exploring, it is worth considering near the beginning of the course what your inspiration is, as this will help you to keep a motivation and drive throughout your studies. For me, when I write, I have the works of Rosa Luxemburg (2004) or George Orwell (1946) swimming around my mind. Both inspire me as to why to write:

When I was studying (a long time ago when I was young and handsome), and in my work now (where I am old and greyer) these words were, and remain a great inspiration. They don't have to be your drive, and writing, as we will see later, isn't the sole aim of your studies, but understanding the impetus for your work is essential. So, before we get too far into the book, have a think about what it is that brought you to do a degree in Media and Communications. It might be to challenge working practices, to question the way women or certain groups of people are treated in the media industry, or you wanted to know about how the way we communicate affects our lives. It might be to learn how to better run a company, or push into new fields and new markets. It might be that you want to explore ethics in AI or develop a deeper understanding of the philosphical underpinnings of Media and Communications. Or maybe another year of access to the cheap student bar. Take a moment to think about what brought you here, to these studies, and make some notes in the box below. Your motivation may change over the course of your degree, but it is good to have a starting point.

I am doing this degree because…..

Whatever you have written above, a Masters degree is designed to give you a chance to find, and then explore your passions in depth, with the guidance of your lecturers and tutors. To do this effectively though, it is essential to know how you will manage your time, to look after yourself and plan your studies to ensure you have the space to read, write, think, experiment and take joy from your university experience.

Managing your time

There have been many embarrassing moments in my life, but one that I am willing to share with you, here in these pages, is about the time I downloaded an audio book about how to manage time better. It was a free download (the best things in life are free to download), and I was eager to find out how I was going to reorganize my life to ensure I met my deadlines, attended parties, slept and kept my sanity. That podcast sat on the desktop of my laptop for months. A note to listen to it appeared on my to-do list. The podcast got transferred to a new laptop, and then to another new laptop. Eventually, it was deleted, unheard, advice unheeded, and leaving a rather strange sense of failure.

Clearly the podcast was too long, the daunting task of sitting down to listen to it for a whole 20 minutes(!) was just too much to bear and so it never happened. Throughout your studies there are going to be many of these kinds of moments, moments when you think, I haven't got time for that now, so I will save it for later. You may even be thinking that about this book. A Masters degree is a huge undertaking, and so it is worth thinking carefully about how to carve out some space for both reading and writing as well as other aspects of studying – and while we are here, let's carve out some space for parties, socializing, networking and enjoying the place in which you are studying – after all, you have already read a handful of pages of this book, so you deserve it.

As with all aspects of academic work, the first job is to identify the problem, only then can we seek a solution. So, take a few minutes to think about the biggest time management issues you have. Perhaps there is a specific time when things didn't work, perhaps there is something that is always a distraction? Write some of your ideas down in the space below – don't worry, you have time.

My time management issues are:

There are lots of reasons that we might struggle to manage our time well, and you may have identified slightly different ones to those which I will mention here, but many of our time management issues come from the same kind of place, the place where podcasts about time management go to die. That is, that we worry that we don't have time to finish something, and so we don't start it. And then, after many weeks have passed we find the deadline has appeared and we still have to do the work, but now, WE DON'T HAVE TIME!

The best way around this is to think of your degree as a job (sorry that sounds boring). Not a real job of course, but a job where you get to read and discuss ideas all day, a job where you get to make suggestions and put forward ideas and a job that often comes with lots of great social benefits (sounds better). It is though nonetheless a job (sorry).

How do we get ourselves into that state of mind? Well, we could get up each morning and put on a tie (or not) and fancy shoes and walk to the library for a 9am start and then leave again at 5:30pm, but that isn't really how people work best. People all work a little differently and at different times of the day. Furthermore, you have classes, your sports club, your band plays on Thursdays, and your mum comes to visit every Friday. Whatever it is, things get in the way of a 9–5 approach to a degree. Instead we need to build a custom weekly plan that will help us to keep on top of our work.

Following is a weekly planner to help you with this, and we are going to fill it in step by step using a template to create our own 9–5.

1. The first step is to add your classes onto the timetable. Block these out in one colour.
2. Now add any paid job that you might have (studying is an expensive business).
3. If you have a club or something that you just can't give up, then block this out too.

By now you might have something that looks like that in figure 2.1. We have added all the things that just can't be moved, and that we need to place our independent study around.

Here comes the hard part, now we are going to add in study time. But wait! It is not as simple as just saying all the other parts are study time; that is where things often go wrong. We can't study 24 hours a day, 7 days a week, and without some careful consideration we might be wasting our best working moments. Instead, we need to think carefully about a few things:

- What time of day do you work best?
- Can you get up in the morning?

Time	Mon	Tues	Wed	Thurs	Fri	Sat	Sun
6 - 7							
7 - 8							
8 - 9							
9 - 10						Job	
10 - 11		Lecture		Lecture		Job	
11 - 12		Lecture		Lecture		Job	
12 - 13		Lecture		Lecture		Job	
13 - 14						Job	
14-15	Lecture	Lecture				Job	
15 - 16	Lecture	Lecture		Training		Job	
16 - 17	Lecture	Lecture		Training		Job	
17 - 18	Lecture			Training		Job	
18 - 19						Job	
19 - 20							
20 - 21							
21 - 22							
22 - 23							
23 - 00							

Figure 2.1: Unmoveable events.

- Can you work after class, or are you too tired?
- Can you work late at night?
- If you can work at night, are you likely to get distracted by more exciting plans?

For me, I like to work in the mornings and I know I can't work well after I have given a class as my brain is too tired, so I block out periods of working time that are in the mornings, and so my weekly plan looks more that in figure 2.2.

Note that I still have a good 20 hours of study time in this picture, along with 15 hours of lectures. This makes for a 35 hour week; not even quite a

Time	Mon	Tues	Wed	Thurs	Fri	Sat	Sun
6 - 7							
7 - 8	Study		Study		Study		
8 - 9	Study		Study		Study		
9 - 10	Study		Study		Study	Job	
10 - 11	Study	Lecture	Study	Lecture	Study	Job	
11 - 12	Study	Lecture	Study	Lecture	Study	Job	
12 - 13		Lecture	Study	Lecture		Job	
13 - 14			Study	Lecture		Job	
14 - 15	Lecture	Lecture	Study			Job	
15 - 16	Lecture	Lecture	Study	Training		Job	
16 - 17	Lecture	Lecture	Study	Training		Job	
17 - 18	Lecture		Study	Training		Job	
18 - 19						Job	
19 - 20							
20 - 21							
21 - 22							
22 - 23							
23 - 00							

Figure 2.2: Adding in study time.

full time job. And furthermore, I am always finished my independent study by 6pm, when my brain starts to slow down and often insists I stop writing. Understanding that something that takes me three hours to do of an evening will only take one hour with a fresh brain in the morning really helps me to manage my time. For you it might be different, you might work best at night and need a long time to wake up. The important thing is to take this into consideration in your planning. So, think carefully about when you work best and add this to your chart.

Weekly work planner

Building a custom weekly plan that will help us to keep on top of our work. Add your classes, work commitments and clubs first, then block out space every week to complete assignments and reading – then stick to this, don't try more, and don't do less.

Time	Mon	Tues	Wed	Thurs	Fri	Sat	Sun
6 - 7							
7 - 8							
8 - 9							
9 - 10							
10 - 11							
11 - 12							
12 - 13							
13 - 14							
14-15							
15 - 16							
16 - 17							
17 - 18							
18 - 19							
19 – 20							
20 - 21							
21 - 22							
22 - 23							
23 - 00							

Figure 2.3: Planner.

This is a great start. We have a solid frame work from which to begin. Sticking to this routine will not only help you keep on target, it will also stop you from burning out. The secret is to work at the times you said you would, even in a week with less assignments, and not work when you said you won't. However, we all know that that is easier said than done. There is still always the creeping issue of procrastination. That constant risk of getting nothing done at all. What is to be done about this?

Treat your studies as a day job. That really helped me plan how to read, and save some time for family engagements and part-time work.

Alfonse – MA Media and Development

Procrastination

A degree involves a huge amount of self-discipline, and thus the spectre of procrastination is never far away, but what is it really? And how can you avoid it? Or at the very least keep it at bay for the time you are undertaking your studies? Having a good timetable like that above is a good start, but there are a few other things we can do too, and that is what this section is going to be all about. So, stop watching Netflix, no need to pair up all your socks, your kitchen doesn't need cleaning right this minute, instead let's work on some tactics together, because unlike Mozart, most of us aren't capable of writing the overture to *Don Giovanni* the morning of the premiere (he really did).

First, it is important to know the issue isn't unique to you. All students, lecturers and writers suffer this to some extent. Even famous writers such as Franz Kafka agonized over their writing and how it didn't always come easily, as we can see from these extracts from his diary in 1915.

JANUARY 20, 1915: The end of writing. When will it take me up again?

JANUARY 29, 1915: Again tried to write, virtually useless.

JANUARY 30, 1915: The old incapacity. Interrupted my writing for barely ten days and already cast out. Once Again prodigious efforts stand before me. You have to dive down, as it were, and sink more rapidly than that which sinks in advance of you.

FEBRUARY 7, 1915: Complete standstill. Unending torments.

MARCH 11, 1915: How time flies; another ten days and I have achieved nothing. It doesn't come off. A page now and then is successful, but I can't keep it up, the next day I am powerless.

MARCH 13, 1915: Lack of appetite, fear of getting back late in the evening; but above all the thought that I wrote nothing yesterday, that I keep getting farther and farther from it, and am in danger of losing everything I have laboriously achieved these past six months.

Figure 2.4: Kafka's diary.

So then, what do we do to stave off procrastination, to keep to our study plan and to ensure that we are able to meet all our deadlines and are able to enjoy our time studying without slipping into Kafka's desperation. We all start our studies, as well as New Years, and most new projects, with very high expectations. 'This time', we tell ourselves, 'is the time we will work perfectly'. This plan though, can actually get in the way of our work. Giving so much importance to the work you are about to do can make it much harder to get into the flow, or to stay there. You can become over self-critical and this can stop you from working. One way to try and overcome this is to use the two-goal approach. When our expectations are too high we don't feel comfortable setting realistic goals, we might feel we are not pushing ourselves hard enough. To solve this, we should set ourselves two sets of goals. One is a realistic one, the other is what we might call a stretch goal.

For example, the realistic goal might be to read five articles (or write 1000 words, or edit five minutes of video). The stretch goal might be to read eight articles (or write 1500 words, or edit eight minutes of video). So, if you manage to read five articles, you get that great feeling of achieving your goal, and can rest easy. If, however, you manage more, that is a bonus (Whoop!) This little psychological trick you play on yourself can help you manage the balance between high expectations and achievable goals.

Figure 2.5: Number of articles to read.

Not managing this balance can lead to your passion waning, because not meeting your own high expectations leads to disappointment. To deal with this we succumb to other ideas and start doing things we know we can achieve – like watching a whole boxset in one sitting. This is something that can then become a habit. To avoid this, it is important to remember why the topic interested you when you started it, and even when the topic isn't so interesting to you, it is important to keep going, to push though the desire to stop the project. Look back at your thoughts on your motivations to help you regain that focus. Pushing through the desire to stop, and instead keeping on track with your work (and here comes the science part) actually changes the neurological pathways in your brain, and repeatedly finishing projects rather than dropping them builds up good neural habits that will mean it gets easier and easier to stave off procrastination (Duhigg, 2012). Using your timetable from the previous pages will help with this.

Make your tech a little more humane

Smartphones are great, but they can become a bit of a distraction, but just suggesting you turn if off for a year isn't too helpful. Luckily the Centre for Humane Technology provides us with some great tips about how to take control of our smartphones in a way that means we can still use them, but they won't be competing for our attention. They suggest, turning off notifications that aren't from people, and changing your icons to grey scale, to stop them leaping out at you when you are just checking the time. Try making only the essential apps appear on your home screen, even going as far as making some apps only launchable by typing their whole name. They have loads of other great tips, and also provide a range of apps to help you take control of your smartphone. Go check them out!

humanetech.com/take-control

Despite this, at least once in your studies you are likely to experience burn-out. This isn't writers block, this isn't procrastination, this is that you are totally exhausted. You can limit the chances of this happening by following the advice above, but should it occur there is only one way to solve this, and that is to give yourself a few days rest. This is a tricky one though. Yes, you need to rest, to go for dinner with friends, take long walks, or watch some films. This, though, only works if you truly take a break. You need to not work at all in this time. Do not stare at the screen – trying to work builds up a cycle of guilt, followed by not fully resting, which is again followed by being unable to work. The only way to break this cycle is to stop totally. Decide how long you will need, a few days perhaps, and then step away from all your studies, totally and fully. You will come back with a new passion, and be able to work faster and harder.

The final issue faced by Masters students is just being too distracted. And of course you are. A new city, new friends, new ideas and thousands of adventures to be had, inside and outside your mind. You may also be distracted by being sick, having to take a job, looking after children, or many other aspects of life. However, unless you are taking a total break to recover from burn-out, you should try and keep some sort of work going. Continue to read books related to the subject you are studying and keep a notebook to jot down ideas, even if you don't have time to work on them right now, you will later, and this will keep your mind working on the issues you are studying. It is also good to adjust your writing schedule to consider unavoidable distractions as they occur. Learning your best way of learning is an ongoing process and will evolve during the year, so keep your working schedule current to help you find the right times to grow into being a fantastic scholar and researcher. Novelist Chinua Achebe says:

Chinua Achebe

Types of assessment

Before we get too far into the book, it is probably worth a short note on the types of assessment you might be asked to undertake. Generally assessments fall into two types, those for formative, and summative. You will probably hear your lecturers talk about these, and they will likely have these names in module and course handbooks. But what are they and what does it mean for you? Well, in simple terms one goes towards your grade, and the other doesn't. Why would you do an assessment that doesn't add to your grade? Well the formative assessments, without a mark, are designed to help you and your tutor discover how your learning is going, what things might need improving, and where you could seek help. It also helps tutors to change the direction of a class if there is something that lots of people do not understand. Summative assessments on the other hand, are designed to test your skills and knowledge and to give you marks. Both are really important, and both should be taken seriously. Formative work really helps with reflection, too (see chapter 6).

Other study tips

Before we get right into the nitty gritty of doing your degree over the next eleven chapters, let's look at some general tips to help you sustain your studies, many of these will also help you in your life in general, and the workplace. Whatever your working schedule, you must take regular breaks (perhaps try the Pomodoro Technique, see p. 19). Think about where you are working; try not to work in bed, so you have a separate space to rest. Consider whether you prefer working in the library, the kitchen table, your desk or in a café. Once you know your best working space (this might be different for different types of work), stick to this – I like to do emails and admin work in public spaces, but I need music to write and silence to edit, so I ensure I move around when working on different parts of a project. Also, think about the light and temperature in the room you are working in. Consider spending a little money on a good lamp – Michel Foucault, the French philosopher and social theorist, used to take his own to libraries and lectures. You should also break tasks down into smaller chunks or sub-tasks – there are some pages to help you do this at the end of this book. You can also use technology to help you with this, there are loads of task management apps available, although trying them all out can become a form of productive procrastination, so be careful! One piece of technology you should certainly take advantage of though is your university's Virtual Learning Envionment (VLE). These come in many forms, such as Blackboard or Canvas, but essentially these are all places where content from lectures and assements are collected together. You should ensure you are familiar with these tools, and where resources are located to help your studies flow more smoothly. And finally, eat regularly, and try to eat well, while also enjoying what you eat. Most importantly, drink plenty of water. Your brain needs water to work, so stay hydrated wherever you are working. And always follow the advice of sociologist Theodor Adorno:

THEODOR W. ADORNO

The Media Students' Tool Bag

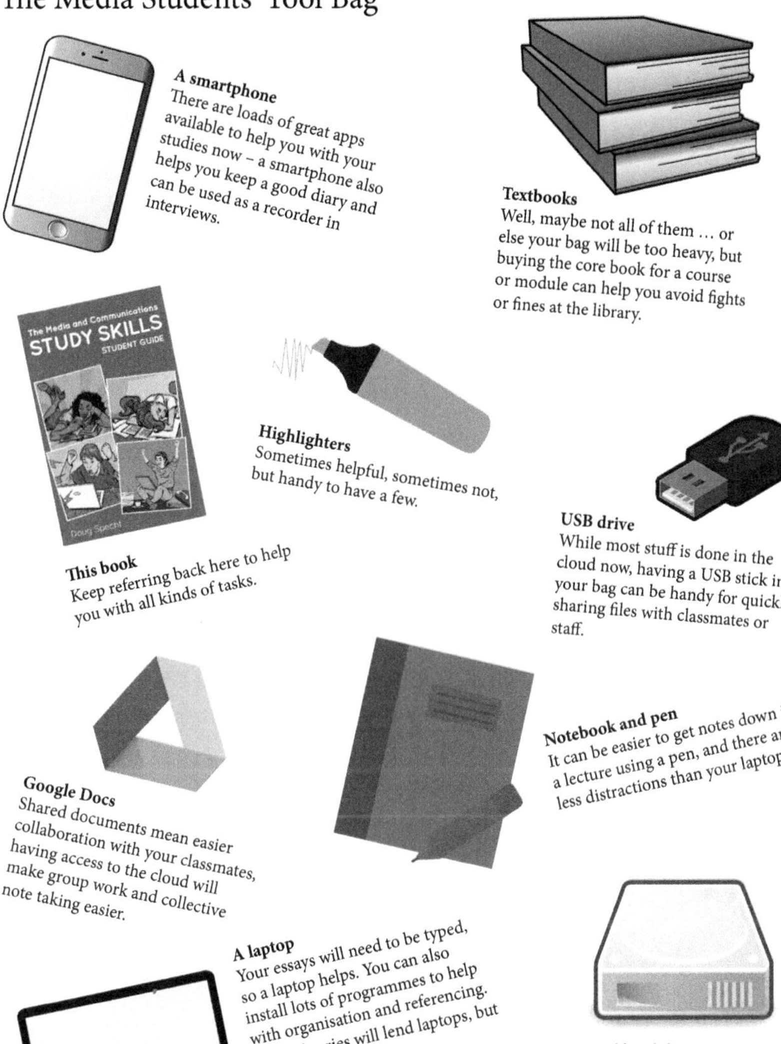

Figure 2.6: The media students' tool bag.

Evernote
Android/iOS/Web, free
A tool that allows you to capture a note or memo in any format (web clip of a product or service review for reference, photo of a business receipt, audio file, or text meeting or handwritten notes).

Dragon Dictation
iOS, free
Have a brilliant thought on that Foucault reading you've been pondering? Don't waste time trying to type it: Use Dragon Dictation to translate your spoken words into text. Just start talking into Dragon Dictation and it'll convert everything for you digitally, which you can paste into other apps, send as an email message, or save it for later.

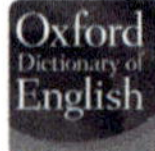

Oxford Dictionary –
Android/iOS, free
The mobile version of the Oxford University Press' Oxford English Dictionary.

RefME –
Android/iOS/Web, free
This nifty app uses your phone's camera to scan a book's barcode and create a citation formatted in MLA, Chicago, or whatever format your school uses.

WhatsApp: If you decide to spend a semester abroad, or if your friends do, stay in touch via the WhatsApp real time messaging service — sans SMS fees. WhatsApp is also useful on the home front: Create customized messaging groups to share texts, audio and images with classmates and study buddies to stay on the same page.

myHomework Student Planner –
Android/iOS/Windows, free
myHomework is a digital student planner that lets you track your classes, homework, tests and projects so you never forget an assignment again.

Google Drive –
iOS/Android, free
Save and store all of your documents online so that your work will be safe if your laptop crashes. You can also work offline and collaborate on a document with your classmates.

Virtual Learning Environment (VRE) apps – iOS/Android, free
Different institutions use different online learning platforms, but most have their own app, which can help you keep track of your timetable and learning resources.

Otter – iOS/Android, free
Record and transcribe lectures and interviews with ease. Free up to 600 minutes every month

Figure 2.7: The apps every media student needs.

TOP TIPS

The Pomodoro Technique is a time management method developed by Francesco Cirillo in the late 1980s. The technique uses a timer to break down work into intervals, traditionally 25 minutes in length, separated by short breaks. These intervals are named pomodoros, the plural in English of the Italian word pomodoro (tomato), after the tomato-shaped kitchen timer that Cirillo used as a university student, when he devised the technique.

Adapted from MyLearnMBA (2017)

Now we have some good working habits under our belt, or in our back pocket, or wherever you are keeping them, it is now time to look at all the aspects of the work you will be undertaking. The following chapters are designed to build upon each other, but you will also be undertaking many of these tasks simultaneously, so it is worth going through the whole book, and then coming back to each section as you need. I'll see you in chapter 3!

References

Duhigg, C. (2012). *The power of habit: Why we do what we do in life and business* (Vol. 34, No. 10). New York: Random House.

Luxemburg, R., Hudis, and Anderson, K. B. (2004) *The Rosa Luxemburg reader*. New York: Monthly Review Press

MyLearnMBA (2017) Manage time with the Pomodoro Technique. [Online] Available from: https://medium.com/@MyLeanMBA/manage-time-with-the-pomodoro-technique-62917906bb3b Accessed 30 January 2019.

Orwell, G. (1946) Why I write. *Gangrel* (Summer).

CHAPTER 3

Listening skills and getting the most from lectures and lecturers

On a Masters course the majority of your learning normally comes from reading – this is why in some places they call it reading for a degree. However, lectures, seminars and group work are a key part of your academic life, and being able to listen in these sessions is a really important skill, and one that we all need to work on – we spend a lot of time only half-listening to each other. We all like to think we are good listeners – bad news though, we aren't. The problem is that most of us think that hearing what is said is the same as listening to what is being said. However, they are very different, hearing is the physical act, the bit that makes the eardrum move, so you know sounds are coming your way, but is is very passive, you can do this in your sleep. Listening on the other hand (ear?) is hearing the sounds with deliberate intention, and that is what we really need when undertaking listening for learning, and becoming an active listener enables you to respond and remember what is being said. So, while you might think that you are a good listener, chances are you could be better. And what's more, knowing how to listen can help you pick up information about what might be in an exam, what your professor wants you to write, or even just a snippet of information to help you get by in your studies or to find opportunities outside the classroom.

Active and focused listening

Communication is sometimes referred to as being a two-way street, and so you will need to be able to look both ways before stepping into it. In the next chapter we will look at how you can contribute to conversations, by expressing your thoughts, feelings and opinions clearly and effectively, but first, let's look in the other direction and explore some ways of listening that will help you get

---

How to cite this book chapter:

Specht, D. 2019. *The Media And Communications Study Skills Student Guide*. Pp. 21–26. London: University of Westminster Press. DOI: https://doi.org/10.16997/book42.c. License: CC-BY-NC-ND 4.0

the most from those around you, bearing in mind the words of professor of linguistics, Deborah Tannen:.

DEBORAH TANNEN

The good news is you can improve your listening skills through practice, and it gets much easier with time. The key to focused listening is simple, don't get distracted! And then make a real effort not just to hear what the person is saying, but to listen to what their message is. This will make them want to keep talking, will show them you are following what is happening, and that you are interested (which is something you should be doing, even if you aren't that interested). You don't have to agree with everything they say, in fact at university you will listen to lots of things you disagree with, but you should appreciate the experiences and perspectives of the people you are working with – be they classmates or lecturers. Active listening goes a step further, and enables you to clarify what is happening and which ideas are being shared . This will help you avoid mistakes like submitting on the wrong day, or worse on the wrong topic, just because you misheard something. This is of course not just a skill that is useful in class, but is also hugely important in all aspects of life.

In order to do really good focused listening you must pay attention, give the speaker your undivided attention, and acknowledge the message. You can do this by, looking at the speaker directly (but don't stare creepily, else you will put them off) and by putting aside distracting thoughts – this includes switching off your phone, a vibration in the pocket often sends our minds wandering. Before you arrive into the conversation too, don't already mentally prepare a rebuttal, instead be open to the ideas, even if you disagree. It is also important that the speaker also knows that you are listening, so show them that you're listening! You can also use body language and gestures to show you are paying attention, things like nodding occasionally help, but also smile and use other facial expressions, and keep your posture open (no folded arms!). Encourage the speaker to continue with small comments like 'yes', and 'uh huh'. You can also build on this further, and become a more active listener, by providing feed-back. As a listener, your role is to understand what is being said, so clarify ideas using phrases like, 'what I'm hearing is,' and 'sounds like you are saying,' are great ways to reflect back.

Figure 3.1: Appreciative listening phrases.

Ask questions to clarify certain points, 'what do you mean when you say'; 'is this what you mean?' As you are doing this though you should also avoid making quick judgments – interrupting is a waste of time because it frustrates the speaker and stops you from fully understanding their message. So, let the speaker finish each point before asking questions. When they have finished speaking then you can respond. Active listening is about respect and under-standing. You are gaining information and perspective. You add nothing by attacking the speaker or putting them down. This doesn't mean you shouldn't be honest, but also assert your opinions respectfully. A simple rule, for all life perhaps, is to treat the other person in a way that you think he or she would want to be treated.

Julian Treasure (2017), author of *How to be Heard*, and a number of other books, came up with his own way of being an appreciative listener, something that he called RASA. In Sanskrit the word means 'juice, essence or taste' or something that evokes an emotion or feeling in the reader or audience, but that cannot be described. That sounds like the kind of thing we need. Let's see how it helps us think about listening to people when they are presenting complex or challenging ideas:

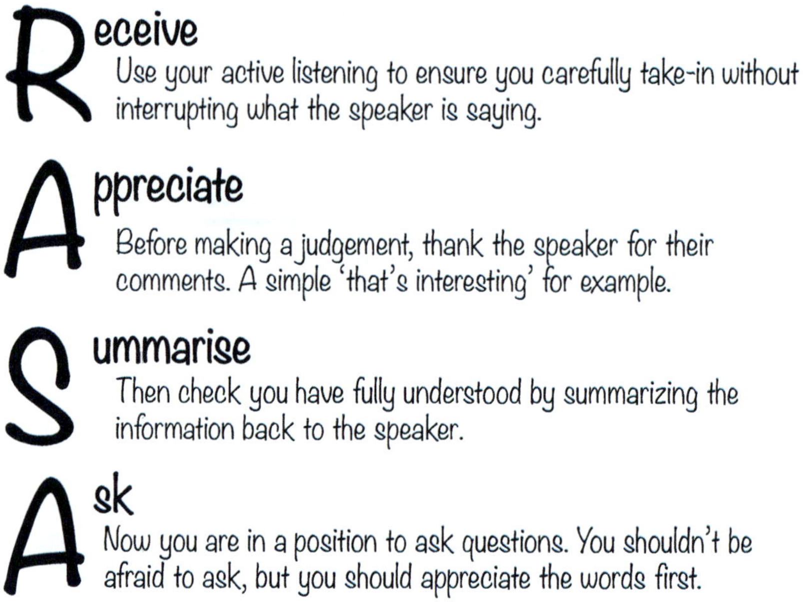

Receive
Use your active listening to ensure you carefully take-in without interrupting what the speaker is saying.

Appreciate
Before making a judgement, thank the speaker for their comments. A simple 'that's interesting' for example.

Summarise
Then check you have fully understood by summarizing the information back to the speaker.

Ask
Now you are in a position to ask questions. You shouldn't be afraid to ask, but you should appreciate the words first.

Figure 3.2: RASA.

You can watch Julian Treasure's TED Talk about RASA online for free:

http://www.ted.com/talks/julian_treasure_ 5_ways_to_listen_better

Nonverbal gestures

Beyond our words and comments, nonverbal gestures are also hugely important in focused listening. In many ways, listening is characterized more by what is not done, than what is done. There are lots of clues as to what the speaker or listener is communicating, and not just words, so you need to try and spot these too. Your tutors will be giving all kinds of signs to you as they speak – some they know they are doing, others they don't – but learning to read these could give you some good insights. Look for waving arms, some lecturers

Figure 3.3: Look out for the subtle signals your lecturers give through non-verbal gestures

gesticulate all the time and look like they are trying to land an aircraft, but they all tend to make quite sharp hand actions when they are saying key things, so watch for those.

Key ideas are often followed by a longer pause in speaking, and if you are lucky, some repetition. They might even be a bit louder. Professors are often accused of being mumblers – so listen for the moments of real clarity, these are the bits they really want you to know. Lecturers will also often walk towards the front of the stage or room when making key points, so look for that too. Don't get too hung up on these movements though, remember to listen and to note down the key points (see the next chapter), but do ensure you pay attention to phrases like 'firstly', 'importantly', and 'this is key', they aren't accidental, they are signs pointing you to the most important information – come to think of it, it is a bit like landing a plane… look for the directions!

Use pen and paper when listening to lectures and taking notes, rather than typing on your computer. Writing is more effective, requires active listening and facilitates memorization. Using your computer instead can be extremely distracting (especially if you're connected to the internet) and impede active involvement in the lecture.

Maria – MA Media Campaigning and Social Change

You also need to think about your own non-verbal communications. You should avoid sending out negative nonverbal gestures, or others will feel you are uninterested, disrespectful or rude. Unfortunately, there are hundreds of potentially inappropriate nonverbal gestures, and these can change depending on the situation (or not) and culture. Some basic ones though might be; entering the room/situation late without an apology or valid reason – obviously this can be tricky in a large lecture theatre, and shouting sorry across a full auditorium might be worse than being late, so instead send an email later. Avoid fidgeting or making distracting physical movements, or yawning, looking around the room or off into the distance. Also, and this one seems obvious, but often happens, avoid multitasking, (e.g. checking your phone), none of us are as good at multitasking as we think we are, and most things will wait until after we have finished listening.

As we can see, listening is a hugely important skill at university, and in life generally. It is well worth taking some time to practice this skill and ensure that you have it mastered. Some conscious effort in class and meetings will make a world of difference, after all as essayist Henry David Thoreau reminds us:

HENRY DAVID THOREAU

This is something he probably didn't get much chance to practise during his two years in the woods of Massachusetts – but good academic advice!

As we said right at the start, Media and Communications is all about people, good communication and an ability to listen are essential both in class, and when you head out into the workplace. So, worth practicing your active listening skills – you can always make them better!

Reference

Treasure, J. (2017) *How to be heard: Secrets for powerful speaking and listening.* Coral Gables, FL: Mango.

CHAPTER 4

Reading, desk research, taking notes and plagiarism

'I know I have read that somewhere!'; 'Where is it?'. 'AHHH, I'll never find it again!'. There is nothing more frustrating than not knowing where an idea came from, or the book your best quote is borrowed from. You get tempted to include it anyway, but without a proper reference you know you shouldn't, so instead you leave it out – what a disaster! It was, without doubt, the highlight of your essay. It is often during reading and notetaking that mistakes are made that can lead to these issues, or to accusations of plagiarism, a serious offence that may cause you to fail an assignment. In this chapter, we are going to help you ensure that the Academic Misconduct Board get to put their feet up, rather than chasing you. We will look at notetaking when reading, the basics of referencing systems, and some referencing tools, because as poet and writer Edgar Allan Poe (1844) reminds us:

Edgar Allan Poe

How to cite this book chapter:
Specht, D. 2019. *The Media And Communications Study Skills Student Guide*. Pp. 27–45. London: University of Westminster Press. DOI: https://doi.org/10.16997/book42.d. License: CC-BY-NC-ND 4.0

Reading scholarly articles or academic books can be challenging, sometimes it feels like the author doesn't want you to understand what they are saying. This is because these texts are usually written for academics in a specific discipline rather than for a general audience. These texts often use jargon (subject specific words) and assume prior knowledge, which you might not have at the start of your studies, but you will (we hope) by the end. Scholarly reading, though, is usually not as difficult as it first seems. You may not understand everything in an academic text, but you can learn to recognize major *road signs* to help you find your way through it.

To get started, the first thing is to note the difference between reading for pleasure and reading academically:

Reading for pleasure	Academic reading
You can choose to read what you want.	Have to read in an active purposeful manner.
It's up to you what kind of texts you choose and why you choose them.	The things you choose to read have to be seen to be 'good' quality or from trusted sources.
You don't have to think about what you are choosing if you don't want to.	You have to evaluate, question, compare and reflect on the value of the sources you are reading and thing about what it is possible to say about them.
You can choose to read when and where you like.	You will have often have to read for the purposes of producing particular types of knowledge, in particular ways, for particular audiences.
You could choose to read the same things day in, day out.	You will have to be able to work with a range of different sources in order to produce particular types of knowledge.

(Escott, 2017 *cited by* @Hemmanony, 2017)

This doesn't mean that academic reading can't be pleasurable, fun and social, it just requires you to think a bit more about the purpose of the text, who the author is, and the audience is was written for. It also involves considering the text's relevance to you, and your studies – and maybe thinking about why your professor asked you to read it… it's not to punish you, I promise! Let's take a look at each of these in turn.

When reading academic texts, first think about the **audience**. Academic texts are often written for other academics, but which ones? One clue is to look at where the article is published and to think about who reads that publication. This will tell you about some of the prior knowledge they might think you have – but it doesn't mean you should disregard the paper if you don't have that knowledge, instead, look at **the title**. The title will tell you the main topic. Academics love long titles; some seem to be longer than your dissertation. While they would make awful novel titles, they are great for you because good academic titles tell you everything. They often come in two parts, separated by a colon. The part before the colon is the fun bit, to draw you in. The bit after the colon does the work, and tells you more about the focus of the article – Fun at the front, work at the back.

Now that we have a rough idea who the audience is, what the article might be about, and the prior knowledge it assumes we have, we know how easy or hard it will be to read. Now it is time to read it carefully keeping in mind **your own purpose**. You might feel like you are not the intended audience, but there is a reason you are working with this text, especially if the reading was assigned by your professor. If you have chosen the text yourself, think about why you chose this reading and decide if it is the text you need or if you should put it to one side and move on to something else. A key thing to learn is the difference between discarding something that is not relevant, and discarding something that just feels too hard.

The good news though – about time we had some – is that in academic reading you don't need to read a text from start to finish (Phew!). Most academic papers contain the same basic parts, and we can look for key information using those. Try looking at the **abstract** which summarizes the text and usually appears at the beginning of an article or book chapter. Not all academic texts have abstracts, but those that do tell us everything about the paper – they would be useless on a murder mystery book because they would tell us who done it, but they are great on academic papers, because they tell us the conclusion without reading everything. The **introduction** also summarizes the text and the main idea, but in much more detail. It also tells us why we should care (and you should, people have spent a lot of time on this work) about the research, how it fits with the 'bigger picture' and gives an overview of what is coming. **Sub-headings** too are useful, after reading the introduction, read all the section headings to give yourself more idea of the shape of the article and the direction it will take you. You might then want to skip straight to the **conclusion** (this isn't cheating). The conclusion can help you make sure you understood the introduction. Now you've looked at these parts, you should have a good idea of the main arguments in the text, and you can decide how much energy to give to different parts of the text as you start to *read critically*.

Reading critically

It is important to read critically. These are words you will hear time and again – but trying to get someone to explain what this means is near impossible. For many professors, it is a skill that has been honed over hundreds of years (they are that old), and when something becomes second nature it can become hard to explain. So, what is it? Well, critical reading requires you to evaluate the arguments in the text (not much clearer), to distinguish fact from opinion, and to try and see both sides of the arguments made by the author (a little clearer). You also need to be aware of your opinions as you are reading, so you can evaluate it honestly. The main idea of critical reading is to evaluate the evidence or arguments presented; to spot any limitations in the design of the study, and to decide how much you accept the authors' arguments, opinions, or conclusions. Remember, all writers have a reason for writing, and will emphasize details that support their opinion. There are three simple things to do, *Question, Evaluate, Locate* (finally it is simple);

| **Question** | **Evaluate** | **Locate** |
what the author says	what the author says	the author in the discipline
❏ What assumptions does the author make? ❏ Do you think these assumptions are correct? ❏ Are the stages of the argument clear and logical? ❏ Are the writer's conclusions reasonable in the light of the evidence presented?	❏ How do the conclusions relate to other similar research? ❏ Are you persuaded by what the author says? Why/why not? ❏ If someone asked your opinion of the author's viewpoint, what would you say? ❏ How will you use what the author says in your argument?	❏ What is the authors position on the issue? ❏ How is the author's argument different or similar to those of other experts on this subject? ❏ How does the author's argument and position fit with what you already know? ❏ Does the author's argument belong to a particular school of thought (e.g. Marxism, Feminism)?

Adapted from Godfrey (2018).

It is important to remember that *critical* here doesn't mean to criticize, the aim of critical reading is not to just find what's wrong, but instead you need to evaluate. It is just as useful to find a really good argument you like, as it is to find one you think is weak – and you can write about both in a critical way by following the steps above – Question, Evaluate and Locate.

Surviving a super long reading list

At universities in the UK it isn't unusual for each of your modules to have reading lists of 30 or more books, articles or other texts. And in some modules, this can be even more, with 10 or more required and recommended readings each week or class. How are you meant to cope with this? Even with the best time management, it becomes impossible to read so many texts each week. So, what to do? Here is the good news, you aren't expected to read all the things on your reading list, instead you need to be selective about what is most useful to you and your learning, in that moment. One of the reasons modules and courses have so many texts is to allow you to find your own way through the ideas. But how will you know which are the most important, and which are right for you? Well, you might find that your readings are split into required and recommended, you should always do the required, and you should aim to do at least some of the recommended. Try these methods for choosing what you will read.

It is normally best to start by reading a text which gives a general overview of the topic. This will help you to put everything else into context and will also give you some ideas about the main debates. You could also look at the references provided in that text to help you find other readings that are related. Books with words like 'introduction', 'handbook' or 'guide' in the title might be the best place to start your reading.

The next texts to consider for your reading, and generally learning, are those written more recently, or which have been written by the big shots in the field you are studying. Even recent books will generally refer back to the older theories so you will be getting up to date with ideas, and also connecting with the historical ideas that led them to reach their conclusion. You can always go back to read the original, older, texts if you need more clarification later.

Finally, there might be some much older texts on your reading list. These are normally written by the most prominent people in your field, and they offer a good cornerstone to your work, but often they will also be referenced in newer books. You will be expected to be aware of current thinking and research in your subject area, for this reason, books that were written a long time ago can be problematic if their theories have changed or been debunked, but if your tutor asked you to read it, there is probably a good reason. You should always be careful to check that what you are reading is relevant to your topic too, time isn't always on our side, so while it might be interesting to read about social media in China, if your essay is about social media in the USA, you might find that the theories and research are too different for it to be useful (at this time).

It's not all about books and journals

But you're a cool person who doesn't just read books and journal articles, you follow authors on Twitter and learn about theory from lectures on YouTube. You listen to podcasts, you write about films, and you seek industry data from

MARSHALL MCLUHAN

informed and exciting databases. All of these things are possible too. The principles in this chapter are the same though. You will need to evaluate the quality of the source, and make choices about which materials are relevant. You will also need some extra notes about the things you listen to, read or watch. Always note down who is speaking, who is directing, who produced it and when. Also note down when you watched it, and the URL. Also consider taking screenshots from social media as things sometime get deleted. Additionally, you may need to think about how reliable a source is. The majority of the books and journals you read will have been peer reviewed, meaning other academics have read it before publication and agreed that it is good enough, and balanced enough to be published… and while your library will have subscriptions to some of the resources below, which means we can trust them more, the same is not true for the majority of open internet content, so you will need to be a little more careful. Below are some tips for some of the additional mediums you might be using:

Requires library subscription

Statista is a huge database, that contains more than 1,000,000 statistics on more than 80,000 topics from more than 22,500 sources (wow!). This has helped to make it one of the most successful databases in the world. This one isn't only media and communications though, in fact is covers 170 different industries. This can make it a really useful resource for giving you context for your essays, providing evidence for ideas or even for sparking thoughts about what you might like to study for your dissertation. And despite their name, they don't just provide statistics, they also have data on market forecasts, white paper studies, dossiers, industry reports, digital market outlooks and consumer market outlooks. The other great thing is they also help you reference their information. You will need to check your library to find out how to login through your university. www.statista.com

Requires library
subscription

Factiva is another huge database, this one is owned by Dow Jones and Company and brings together access to more than 32,000 sources (such as newspapers, journals, magazines, television and radio transcripts, photos, etc.) from nearly every country worldwide in 28 languages, including more than 600 continuously updated newswires. This makes it a really fantastic resource for finding out what is happening right now! Again, this database is useful for background information, but can also provide information for analysis for research projects. As with Statista you will need to check with your library about how to login to get access for free: www.dowjones.com/products/factiva

Requires library
subscription

Box of Broadcasts (BoB) is a cheeky way to avoid your Netflix subscription… well almost. BoB (as it is known) is a database of UK television programmes. It gives you the chance to watch, record and store programmes or extracts from them, into your own online play list, which unlike other places, it lets you keep so long as you need. It also contains transcripts of many programmes and some further information about channels and shows. There are over 2 million broadcasts available, so if you are working on anything related to broadcast it is a real must have resource. Ask your library about how to access: learningonscreen.ac.uk/ondemand

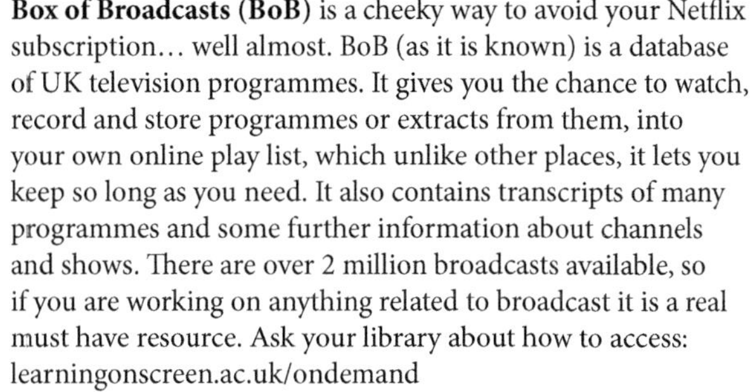

Requires library
subscription

Mintel is a market research firm, that provides databases, analysis, and forecasts to subscribing clients and to students in participating university libraries (that's you!). Mintel undertake a range of activities, but perhaps most useful for you and your studies and the online reports containing consumer research and analysis, market drivers and market forecasts. They also have a 'trends' section that examines emerging marketing, social and cultural trends, which again can provide inspiration for research projects, or up to date background information as part of the context your essays and studies. Furthermore, Mintel also publishes opinions from Mintel analysts, which can be very informative, if a little subjective. Ask your library for more: www.mintel.com

Requires library
subscription

Mediatel is a data and analysis tool that brings together industry data, mostly to help companies plan and make decisions. It is also really useful for media and communications students as it provides information about the circulation of newspapers and magazines, as well as information on the readership of these publications. It also gives us listening and watching figures for radio and TV, as well as information on advertising costs, the demographics of viewers. This information is again great for background and context, as well as for sparking potential research ideas for your dissertation when the time comes. Speak to the library about how to access: mediatel.co.uk

Office for
National Statistics

Free and open

The **Office for National Statistics** is a database of statistics about the UK. Other countries also have similar databases, which you may need if your work isn't UK based. But it is a great example of a database that can be used to provide context to your work. The data held by ONS is produced in a way that makes it easy to compare with other societies and economies. ONS data is produced through a combination of a decennial population census, samples and surveys and analysis of data generated by businesses and organisations such as the National Health Service and the register of births, marriages and deaths. Much of the data here is free and downloadable without a subscription – but it is also a trustworthy source of data.

Free and open

YouTube is full of amazing (and some not so amazing) videos and these can be a great help in your studies. From introductions to a subject area or full lectures on a topic, they can really help to round out your learning, and some of your professors may even include them on reading lists. To get the most out of YouTube as a source, set up a Favourites section for the videos you are using, to help you keep a record. Pretty much anyone and anything can end up on YouTube, so it is always worth thinking about who might have made the video and why. I sometimes search for the channel on other platforms to see if anything has been written about them or how they are funded. Remember, there is loads of good stuff out there, but some people are working to an agenda.

Free and open

Twitter can be a great tool for research. Yes, it can help you get a feel for how a certain population is talking about a subject, and this can be useful in your empirical research (See chapter 12), but in relation to your everyday studies you will find that lots of the people on your reading lists are on Twitter. Follow them! They will often be tweeting other things related to your topic and studies, and you may even get to see their newest work before your professor.

podcast

Some free, some
paid for

Like YouTube, **podcasts** can be a great way to get extra information about the topic you are studying. Again, though you need to think carefully about who made it, why they made it and if they might have a bias and agenda they want to prove.

The internet is a wonderful thing, and it is full of useful and amazing resources. But with this abundance comes issues, and it is important that we are careful about what we use from online. You must make sure you are using reliable sources from reputable people. Think about, who is the author, who paid for the work and what is their agenda. Works you access through your library are checked and vetted by staff and should be reliable. For other sources, you should take care, or use them critically.

Notetaking

Notetaking can be a very personal act, for which there are no right and wrong ways to do it. Some people start by using highlighters to mark key words and phrases or they write the main points with coloured pens or underline them with more coloured pens. Some people draw pictures or diagrams. Some draw arrows, lines, brackets, to help join ideas together. Some people copy and paste chunks of text into a working document. These are all suitable methods, the key is to find the right one for you.

Whatever the method you use, it is important not to just copy the text from a book, or to just highlight things. The idea is to make notes in your own words, while keeping your essay title in mind as you are reading, and only write down things that you will need. Of course, you might find information that might be useful for another essay, if you do, make a note of it, but put it to one side for another time.

It is essential you keep notes about what you read, and which notes are about which text, that will help you avoid the horrid situation at the start of this chapter. So, for every set of notes make sure you note down the following points;

❒ Title, author, place and year of publication, publisher; add URL for internet sources
❒ The numbers of the pages you have read

Then ask yourself and make notes about the following:

❒ What are the paper's main research aims/questions?
❒ What is its scope of analysis (e.g. country, timeframe, media sector)?
❒ What is the paper's main claim for value/originality? (i.e. why is the research important and worth doing)
❒ What research methods were employed?
❒ What are the key concepts and/or theoretical framework?

❏ What are its main findings or core argument?
❏ How might this research paper be useful for my own project?

This is all well and good, but what should the notes themselves look like I hear you ask …

– Well, and this is becoming a theme, there is no right answer. What should good notes look like?

*   *   *

Types of notetaking

There are many different ways of taking notes, and the one that you prefer will depend on your own way of visualizing and remembering information. The following are three of the most common types used by students. Try out a few methods and see what works for you.

Linear notetaking	**Spider notetaking**	**Tabular notetaking**
Notes which follow the order of the points made are called sequential or linear notes. They are most commonly used for lecture notes, but can also work for books. **Advantages** ✓ Simple and familiar approach. ✓ Good for listing information. ✓ Good for detail.	A spider diagram way of summarizing the information that you have found in a visual way, with the central theme in the middle and then other key points linked around it. **Advantages** ✓ You can see complex relationships. ✓ New material can be added at any point.	Notes are drawn out on a table to enable you to make quick and easy comparisons between different issues and ideas. **Advantages** ✓ Useful for codifying and categorizing information. ✓ Very detailed. ✓ Good for essay planning. ✓ Useful exam revision style.

Disadvantages		Disadvantages
✗ Order tends to follow the source. ✗ Difficult to go back and insert additional information. ✗ Repetitive format. ✗ Poor at conceptual/big picture level. ✗ Can reduce complex issues to lists and bullet points.	✓ Good for planning essays as you can design various versions without throwing out old ones. ✓ Links between important points are easily seen. ✓ Visual nature helps you remember the information. **Disadvantages** ✗ Hard to produce, especially from lectures and they require practice.	✗ Hard to draw out 'on the fly' as you need to know most parameters before you begin.

When you have finished making your notes, read through them, make sure you have all the information you need and that you can read your own notes – it's bad enough trying to read the handwriting of your professor, worse if you can't read your own. And then file them safely and in an organized manner until you need them for writing purposes. And even better, your notetaking isn't just great for helping you learn materials, good notekeeping also helps you with your referencing.

Referencing

Referencing is one of those tasks that most people hate, find rather tedious, and also often get wrong, which is hardly surprising given the million different referencing styles. This is frustrating for everyone, but it is one of the most important parts of academic writing. Almost all of the work you produce, even in your dissertation, is about showing your lecturers that you have read widely and understood the texts that you have been reading (at least understanding most of it). It may come as a nasty shock to hear that your lecturers often have very little interest in your own opinion, instead they are interested in how you see the opinions of others. So, referencing then serves two equally important roles for you as a student. The first is to give credit for ideas to those who had them, and the second is to show your professor that you have read widely, and well. Every university and publication has some slight differences in the way in which they like the format of referencing (one of the joys of academic life), and you should check your specific style guides to find out what this is, but here we offer some of the general principles of referencing and see why it is important.

Referencing is a game of two halves:

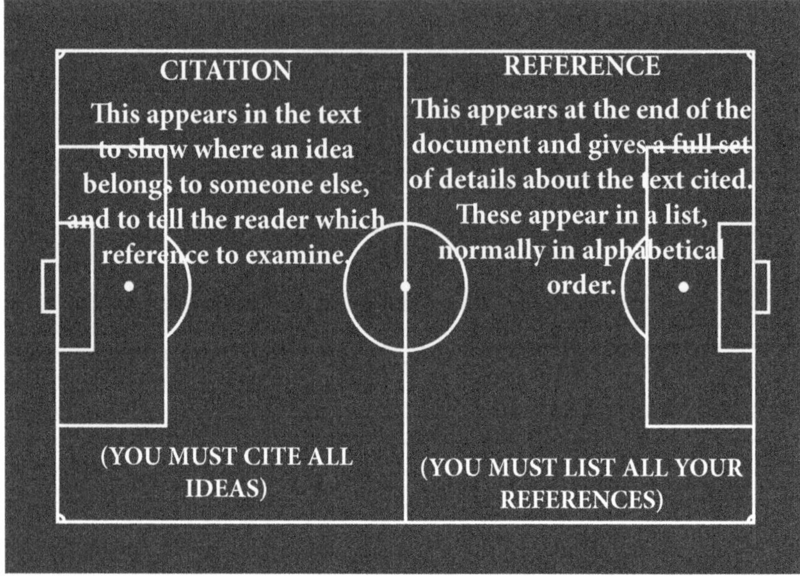

How do we play this game in real life? And avoid being offside (plagiarism). Let's start with the following situation, you have found a wonderful book and it is full of great ideas. You have read it through and have made notes about these ideas. Let's say for the sake of argument that the book is about chickens and their road crossing habits, and that the book was written by Sarah Smith in 2012. The thing you thought was particularly interesting was that chickens cross roads a lot, and you want to state this in your paper. Well, we know this isn't your idea, so we need to tell the reader that you read Sarah's book and that it was her idea. We can do this in a number of ways:

We could *cite* Smith **indirectly**, like this:	Smith (2012) has stated that chickens often cross roads.
Or we could *cite* Smith **indirectly** like this:	Chickens are often found crossing roads (Smith, 2012).

Note that in both these cases we are taking Smith's words and rephrasing them into our own words (see chapter 8), but also notice that is still very clear that it is Smith who had this idea, and it is something that we have read.

Sometimes we read something that is just so amazing, or uses such specific terminology, that is it just impossible for us to rephrase. To share Smith's work that way would require a little more care, as we then need to quote Smith.

We could cite Smith **directly** with a **quote** like this:	'Chickens love the smell of cars' (Smith, 2012: p.23).

Notice that things that are a little different here, we now have quotation marks, and everything between those are exactly the same as how Smith wrote them in her text. We have also added a page number to the citation, this way the reader could go and find the exact same quote themselves from the original source.

And that is basically it for our in-text citations, they really only fall into three types. Of course, there are some variations, such as what happens if there is no author? Or no date? What about if there is more than one author? The handy table below will help with those, but remember you should check the guide from your own institution.

Problem	Solution
There is no page number	Replace page number with: n.p.
There is no date	Replace date with: n.d.
Two authors	List both names (Smith and Jones, 2017).
More than two authors	List the first name, but then et. al. – (Smith et. al., 2017)
The article doesn't have an author	List the name of the publication as the author. The in-text citation and the reference list should match. E.g. (BBC, 2017).

So those are our citations, but that is only half the story, we also need to add this text to our reference list, this is the list of all the articles, books and other things we have cited in our essay or thesis. This comes at the very end of an essay and should be a full list of everything cited (used in the essay) in alphabetical order. Our example might be listed like this:

Smith, S. (2012) Why chickens cross roads. *Journal of chicken studies.* Vol.4(2) p.155–167.

This tells the reader the text is by Smith, it was published in 2012, that it was published by the *Journal of chicken studies*, volume number 4, issue number 2, and that the article started on page 155. This means that anyone reading your work can go back and find this article and read the exact same version as you. This isn't to check up on you, it is because your writing will be so interesting that people will want to go and read further and find out more about the subject.

There are also plenty of other cool things we can do with our citations that will help make our writing rich, interesting and complex – all the things that academic writing should be. We will look at these in depth in other chapters, but you could try things like;

Indirectly citing **3 different authors** who all had similar ideas;

Not all chickens liked the other side of the road (Jones, 2011; Abdul, 2015; Lopez, 2013).

Here, each of Jones', Abdul's and Lopez's texts say something very similar, and we can just include them all in the same citation, using a semi-colon to make it clear they are different texts and not co-authors. Each of the three texts would also then be listed fully in our reference list.

You might see or want to use **other variations** of this, such as;

Chickens are most happy when it is sunny (Conway *et al.*, 2015; Smith, 2012; Mills and Boon, 2014).

Here, the first text has more than two authors, so we write *et al.* (but we name all the authors in the reference list at the end). The second text is just one author. The third text has two authors. All three papers though agree that chickens are most happy when it is sunny. For more on how to bring multiple texts together like this, see chapter 8 on synthesizing.

You must always remember to:

✓ Put your reference list in alphabetical order.

✓ Make sure the order of information in the reference is correct.

✓ Ensure punctuation is exact.

✓ Make sure you are also using the correct typeface and style to match the rest of your document.

Referencing digital media

The tips and tricks above are great, but do they work for other forms of media? Well almost. Referencing systems are always being updated and changed so that they can include other forms of writing, although they don't always keep up with modern technology, and so debates around the right way to cite and reference things like Twitter are still ongoing. What is important to remember is that even a slightly incorrect reference is better than no reference at all. And one that has too much information is better than one without enough. So when you are referencing things like Twitter or YouTube make sure you note down not only the person's name, the year of publication and the name of the video or podcast, etc. but also take a note of user names, URLs, and the exact date of publication. You should check your own libraries resources on referencing to see how your university would like you to reference social media, but here is our recommendation:

In text	In references
(@michaelao, 2019)	@michaelao (March, 2019) "Journalists covering **#Peoples VoteMarch** and thinking about 'balancing' this with Farage, Here's the link to Galtung's piece" https://www.theguardian.com/world/2019/jan/18/johan-galtung-news-principles-journalists-too-negative?CMP=Share_iOSApp_Other … **@BBCPolitics @NickCohen @bbclaurak** [Twitter Post] Available from: https://twitter.com/michaelao/status/1109432533261914112

Online tools for notetaking and referencing

The internet also offers us a huge range of tools for helping you to organize your notes and to help you with your referencing. There are many factors to consider when choosing which one to use, for example, you might be looking for the fastest and easiest option—something that is easy to learn and will let you store all your documents easily. Or you might need something that interacts well with other databases and specific tools you need for the analysis in your work. Either way, let's not forget this: it does need to be free or cheap.

But wait... there's still more!

Use bookmarks and sorted bookmark folders to note interesting things to come back to from the internet. Easy to forget otherwise. Start by creating folders for what's most important. Chrome and Safari seem better to me for this. Sadly, Firefox can be a bit clunky especially on older PCs.

Richard – MA student

Overview of some key resources for digital reference lists and organizing reading (Adapted from University of Toronto, 2019)

	RefWorks	Zotero	Mendeley	EndNote Basic (Web-only)	EndNote Desktop (X8)
How much does it cost?	Many institutions have access for free for their students. Check with your library	Free and open source	Free for everyone	Free	Many institutions have access for free for their students. Check with your library
How does it work?	Web-based interface accessible anywhere	Plugin for Firefox or desktop client which can be linked to Chrome or Safari	Desktop client (Win/Mac/Linux)	Web-based interface. Register through Web of Science. Accessible anywhere.	Desktop client (Win/Mac)
Can I use it on my mobile device?	RefMobile website (free)	Third party apps for iOS & Android (various prices)	iOS app (free)	iPad app (Free)	iPad app (Free)
Can I save citations while I browse?	Yes	Yes	Yes	Yes	Yes
Can I search external databases?	Yes	Limited: ISBN, DOI, or PMID lookup	No (coming soon)	Yes	Yes

Can I automatically grab Pdfs?	Yes: can automatically grab PDFs with citations, can add notes and other attachments, can retrieve citation data for PDFs, can archive web pages	Yes: can organize and annotate PDFs, can retrieve citation data for PDFs	No	Yes: System Find Full Text embeds PDFs to your citations where available.	
Can I run a full text search on my account?	Yes	Yes	Yes	No	Yes
Can I collaborate with others?	Yes: can share folders publicly or privately with RefShare, can share account to collaborate on papers	Yes: can share references through public or private group libraries	Yes: can share references through public or private groups	Yes: can share references privately via groups	Yes: share references with or without PDFs.
What citation styles are available?	3,000+ output styles	2,800+ citation styles (CSL)	2,800+ citation styles (CSL)	3,400+ output styles	5,000+ output styles

Other Options	**Online Options**
While the table above gives us a good overview of some options, there are of course plenty of others out there too, including; BiBTeX; Citelighter; Docear; Qiqqa and ReadCube. As with much of the advice in this book, the secret is to find the one that works best for you, and then stick with it.	There are also lots of free online systems for helping with citations. These tend to only have basic features, but they could be a good place to start, or if you work remotely. Some good ones are BibMe, CiteThisForMe, and EasyBib. Be careful though, not all online tools are reliable, and you should always backup your work on a local disk too.

Plagiarism

Dun Dun Dunnnnnn!!! This word instils fear into students across the land, and if it doesn't, then it really should. It is also often a little misunderstood. Plagiarism itself is defined as 'The practice of taking someone else's work or ideas and passing them off as one's own' (OED, 2012). The word actually comes from the Latin for kidnapper, so you can think of plagiarism as like kidnapping an idea. Universities take this very seriously (both kidnapping and plagiarism, but only one of those is dealt with here), and if you are found to have plagiarized it can result in you being asked to leave the university, and you don't get your money back, and you definitely don't get to wear one of those fancy hats at graduation. The good news is it is actually pretty easy to avoid plagiarizing if you follow a few simple rules:

- ❑ Always use your own words, even if you are worried about your language skills.
- ❑ Avoid using too many quotations – We want to see your own writing too, so look at using paraphrasing and summarizing (chapter 8).
- ❑ Reference your sources using the style of your institution.
- ❑ Don't just copy information from other places, always use your own words when making notes.
- ❑ If you are using a direct quote, make you notes in a different colour, so you remember that those words are not your own, and you can give it the proper citation.
- ❑ If you are going to shorten a direct quote you can indicate this by using three dots inside parentheses (...) where you have removed the words.
- ❑ NEVER submit work written by someone else, or that has been copied from another student.

We can boil all this down to one simple question: Can I submit a paper without citing all sources? The answer is 'No'.

* William Shakespeare, Hamlet, Act III, Scene I, Line 96

References

Escott, H. (2017). Reading vs Academic Reading. [Twitter] Available from: https://twitter.com/Hemmanony/status/915191124939112451 [Accessed February 2019].

Godfrey, J. (2018). *How to use your reading in your essays*. Basingstoke: Macmillan.

OED (2012). *Oxford English Dictionary*. Oxford: Oxford Dictionaries.

Poe, E.A. (1844). Marginalia. *Democratic Review*.

University of Toronto (2019) What's the best citation management software for me? [Online] Available from: https://guides.library.utoronto.ca/c.php?g=250610&p=1671260 Accessed March 2019.

CHAPTER 5

Seminar skills

In seminars there is nowhere to hide – well generally not, occasionally so many students will be packed into one classroom it will be like a game of sardines, but normally seminars are smaller friendlier sessions (they are). They are one of the backbones of learning at university, yet many people find them to be a little daunting. They are much more interactive than a lecture (eek!) and the prospect of having to speak up (ahh!) and share ideas (double ahh!) or to offer critique of our peers (triple ahh!), lecturers (can I leave now please!?) and weekly readings can be very challenging. Worse, in some seminars you will be asked to give formal presentations or engage in group work (call me a taxi!). Yet, for all these concerns, seminars are often the place where most learning happens, and should be a place to test out ideas and push the boundaries of our thinking before writing assessed essays or undertaking exams. With the importance of seminars in mind, this chapter will help you survive seminars, while making useful contributions and giving effective presentations. This chapter will also talk about how to work in groups and how to manage different personalities and skills in group work projects. This will draw upon case studies to help tackle issues in a pragmatic way.

How to cite this book chapter:
Specht, D. 2019. *The Media And Communications Study Skills Student Guide*. Pp. 47–59. London: University of Westminster Press. DOI: https://doi.org/10.16997/book42.e. License: CC-BY-NC-ND 4.0

What is a seminar?

The word seminar comes from the Latin *sēminārium*, which literally means the place for sowing the seed of knowledge, and that is really just what they are. They are designed to provide you with an opportunity to develop your knowledge and understanding of a subject and to practise a variety of academic skills. While they are normally run under the direction of a lecturer or experienced PhD student, the success of the session depends upon the willingness of students (and that includes you) to contribute their own ideas. And your willingness to challenge both your peers and lectures in a constructive and supportive manner. There are six things you can do to help you get the most out of your seminars, and to give the most too.

1. **Be responsible for what happens in the classroom**
   This one might seem obvious from what has been said above, and it is a rather tired cliché to say that you will get out what you put in, however, this couldn't be more true in a seminar. This is your moment to ask all the questions you might have, and to listen to the answers your peers give. Chances are, if you want to ask a question, then someone else will be wondering the same, so pushing yourself to ask is really important. Likewise, the lecturer leading the session is hoping that you will get involved, and so would always rather have 20 questions than a silent room. So come prepared to get stuck in!

2. **Come ready to learn**
   Again, this sounds obvious, but it is more than just remembering to bring a pen – although this is important too. Coming ready to learn means putting everything else in your life to one side for the hour or so of the class. It means doing the readings before the class. It means putting your phone on silent in your bag and closing social media on your laptop. It means more than just being in the room, it means being present. I know there are many other pressures on our lives, partners, family, jobs or even having a cold, but as much as possible, try and leave these things at the classroom door. Much like with active listening, active participation actually requires a great deal of effort and you should be feeling pretty tired by the time the seminar is over… don't forget that pen and notebook too though!

Ask questions!, lots of questions!

Before I go to the lecture, I ask myself what I know about this topic and try to systemize some information I know. During the lecture or seminar, I ask tutors questions to get more clarity or gain more knowledge. After the class, I write a summary (3–5 points) of what I've learned on this topic of the subject.

Mavluda – MA Public Relations

3. **Pick the best seat in the house**

   Where is the best place to sit? Does it really matter all that much, unless you steal the comfy lecturer's chair before they arrive, all the seats are the same, aren't they? No, they really aren't. Where we sit in a room can make a huge amount of difference. Being too close to a radiator or drafty window can make us too hot or cold to learn. Sitting with the sun in our eyes will be a great distraction too. Sitting at the back can make it tempting to disengage or work on other things (we can still see you!). Also consider who you are sitting next to, do they inspire or distract you? Choosing the best seat (for you) can make the seminar so much more pleasurable, and will help you to get the most from sessions.

4. **Take two sets of notes**

   This is surely the most outrageous piece of advice in this whole book! Two sets of notes? *How*? A pencil in each hand? Impossible! That isn't quite what I mean. Instead I mean you should take notes at two different times. The first set you should make while you are in the class. These will of course be quick, short-hand notes scribbled down in a rush. The second set then become even more important, they should be written as soon as the class finishes. This second set of notes is more detailed and written out in full sentences. These notes not only help you consolidate your learning, but they will also serve as better revision notes when you come to exams and writing essays – Don't leave it too long before making the second set, remember (!) we are all pretty bad at remembering things.

5. **Take advantage of the opportunity to connect.**

   This is one of the more fun parts of a seminar. Your seminars are going to be filled with ideas from all over the world, and these will really help expand your thinking (See chapter 12 on shifting perspectives). Better than this though, your colleagues are from all over the world, and will all be moving into working in similar industries to you. So why not use your seminars to also make connections, communicate with people who you may be working with in the future, or even to exchange some invitations to visit other countries on a more sociable basis… or as I like to call them, free holidays!

6. **Be a regular student.**

   Unfortunately, these tips only work if you are in the room, and again it sounds like a bit of a cliché to say you need to go to class, but you really do. Your tutors spend a great deal of time planning the trajectory of lectures and seminars, and so missing one or more of them means you will lose this flow. So, make sure you check your timetable before booking flights during holiday time, and speak with your boss (if you work) to ensure you get to all your seminars – They really are the chance to expand your thinking and get the most from your degree.

Surviving group work

I can almost hear you groan now, that collective sign that echoes around a seminar room when there is the mention of group work. The realization that arguments over workloads, opinions and styles will surely follow. And the sense that all it takes is one person not pulling their weight to pull down everyone's grade is enough to drive you crazy. It doesn't have to be this way, group work can be one of the most fulfilling and rewarding aspects of your studies, and it is also often a very important part of working in the media and communications industry. It takes some extra effort to get it right, but doing so will help you now in your studies and in future work. A good place to start is the six stages of effective group work:

Let's look at each of these more closely.

1. **Principle of individualization**

    Sounds complex, but it just means that everyone learns at their own pace, and in their own way. It is important to realize this as we start group work. Just because we think about or understand the world in a particular way, doesn't mean everyone, or even anyone, else in our group will think or learn in that way.

2. **Goal setting**

    All group work begins with a discussion of objectives/purpose. You should determine what tasks are needed in order to complete the goal of your group work. You should also agree who is best suited to each of these tasks and divide up the responsibility – keeping in mind the *principle of individualization*. Once responsibilities are agreed, deadlines should be set – including any periodical evaluation that might be needed – don't just meet up again at the last minute!

3. Fact finding
This part is often something done solo, and that isn't a bad idea. Allowing each member of the group to gather the data they have been assigned means a range of opinions about that information will also be brought to the table. However, do be empathetic to workloads and learning styles as you assign who will research what.

4. Active listening
When you meet up with your group again, it is really important to engage in active listening as others present what they have found. Reserve your judgement until they have presented their ideas and remember the shape of your project is built upon multiple ideas and should not be shoe-horned into preconceptions. Use some RASA to help with this process (See chapter 6).

5. Production
Only now can you actually begin the process of producing any solid work. Just like all work the collective planning process will help you to produce much better work together. Again, return to the principle of individualization as you assign tasks in the production of your final project output.

6. Evaluation
This should be an ongoing process, but once production comes to an end you should measure the quality of the groups experience in relation to the objectives of the task. This will help to ensure you have reached the goal to the best of the group's _collective_ ability.

The role of empathy

The greatest way to solving any issues with group work is by taking an empathetic approach. Empathy is at its simplest is an awareness of others' feelings, needs and concerns – and this is linked to individualization. While 'empathy is intuitive', comedian Tim Minchin (2013: n.p.), reminds us that it is 'something we can work on and get better at'. Look at the case study below and we can see how it might help in group work.

Tom, Mohammad and Xi are working on a group project. They have all been doing research for a week or so, and are now going to bring in their work. When the group meets up Tom hasn't brought anything with him. Mohammad and Xi get really angry at Tom and start shouting at him. No work gets done during the session. They call it quits and decide that Tom needs to do his work before they meet again. A week later they are set to meet, but now Tom doesn't even turn up. Mohammad and Xi are even more annoyed and complain to the teacher that the task is unfair.

What could they have done differently?

How might this have worked if they had employed some empathy.

When Tom arrived with no work, they might have started by asking him if everything was ok – often there is a reason that people haven't done their work. If they had done this, they would have found that Tom was having to look after his child this week. He had been trying to do the work, but just hadn't managed to and was embarrassed about it. A second meeting might still need to be arranged, or workloads changed, but shouting and being angry meant that Tom also didn't want to come to the next meeting, and the work stopped being a priority. A little empathy might have saved complaints and embarrassment.

MARK TWAIN

of time. Even a one-slide presentation can run over time if not practised, and a 40-slide presentation can end up too short when nervous. So, use as many slides as you need to follow the above rules, and then follow the rules below to ensure good timing.

*   *   *

So now we have the rules for making a good presentation, we need to think about how we present ourselves too. Dale Carnegie (2017/1936), author of *How to Win Friends and Influence People*, once said that:

DALE CARNEGIE

And he isn't wrong, but we can try to ensure that our presentations are the best possible by doing a little bit of preparation of ourselves, and thinking about how we approach the speech.

Of course, you will always start with plenty of research. A presentation, just like everything else you do, requires careful planning and preparation. Make sure you are well versed in the subject that you are going to be presenting on, keep in mind the three-step model from the top if this section to help ensure your presentation moves people to your goal.

You should then make some notes on small cards – use cards so they don't flap with nervous hands, and keep them to bullet point notes as a prompt; there is nothing worse than listening to someone simply read from a sheet of paper – bullet point notes will help keep you more natural.

And now, practice! Make sure you read through your presentation aloud (with any visuals). If possible, get a friend to help with this and to give you some tips, or try videoing yourself so you can see how well you do. Practice will mean you don't need to use the cards so much, and this will help you to feel more confident.

Now, we have a presentation and we know what we will say, how do you deliver it? Well, the delivery starts before we open our mouths. Ensure you arrive in good time for the presentation. Enter the room or approach the stage with a smile, this will help relax your audience, and will produce endorphins that will help you relax too – no need for a shot of whisky, just a smile will do. Be sure to introduce yourself before you start talking. And as you proceed through your talk keep your body language open – don't fold your arms or hide behind a lectern screen or your notes – and make eye contact with people in the room. If you are worried about this, then look at people's foreheads, they will feel like you are looking and them, and they will engage with your talk. Make sure you don't stare at one person, though; you don't want people to think you're creepy.

Think about how you use your voice, slow deliberate sentences are good to make points clear, but become dull if the whole talk is slow. Keep an eye on your time, and ensure that you reach a strong conclusion – leave this up as your last slide, so people can see it during questions. Don't then run away, but thank the audience for listening, accept any applause, and then smile as you leave the stage. If it is an assessed talk you may be given feedback right away, so be prepared to take some notes or to answer questions before you leave.

We all get nervous giving presentations, the difference between those who let the nerves get the better of them and those who don't, comes in the preparation, and for the most part in the research. Before you make any presentation be clear about what you want people to take away at the end of the *show*; remember as Lilly Walters has said 'The success of your presentation will be judged not by the knowledge you send but by what the listener receives'. And always heed the advice of philosopher Hannah Arendt:

Hannah Arendt

Summary

Seminars ask you to engage with a huge range of activities. We have covered some of those here, including how to be an active member of the class, how to engage in group work, and how to give presentations, both in a seminar and beyond. You may also be called upon to undertake other activities too, so keep an open mind as you attend your seminars and be ready to engage. Your seminars are the very best place to learn. They give you a chance to try out new ideas, to challenge yourself, to push the limits of your thinking and to practise new skills. They are also the place where you can ask questions and clarify points with your lecturers and classmates – as well as plan some exciting futures together – so make you take full advantage of every seminar.

References

Carnegie, D. (2017 [1936)). *How to win friends and influence people.* New York: Pocket Books.

Kangas, G. (2012). Giving presentations worth listening to. TEDxEMU [Online] Available from: https://www.youtube.com/watch?v=NUXkThfQx6A. Accessed March 2019.

Minchin, T. (2013). Occasional Addresses [Online] Available from: https://www.timminchin.com/2013/09/25/occasional-address/ Accessed February 2019.

Turkle, S. (2010). Interview Sherry Turkle. PBS Frontline [Online] Available from: https://www.pbs.org/wgbh/pages/frontline/digitalnation/interviews/turkle.html Accessed March 2019.

Developing a reflective approach to learning

So, you have made it to chapter 6! Well done! You must have your procrastination under control. You might be wondering how we have made it all the way to chapter 6 hardly mentioning essay writing. Sure, we have looked at notes, but not how you turn those into an essay, that's what you're here for, isn't it? Well maybe you are, but a Masters degree is about a lot more than writing. And before we can get good at writing at this level we have to master (get it?) a few other things along the way. Over the next few chapters I'm going to show you the mantra of 'think – read – think – write'. But first, a few words on reflection.

The idea of reflection exercises often makes people worried, and you have probably already thought about skipping this chapter (I knew I shouldn't have told you, you don't need to read a whole academic book). But, actually, reflection is a natural human activity and we tend to reflect on our daily lives, our successes and failures, relationships and careers whether we like it or not. Often these things occur at 3am and keep us awake, but some structured reflection can help us with our studies and keep away the night-time worries – who would have thought a book on studying would also help you to sleep! Reflection is important as it enables us to learn from our experiences – both our failures and successes. It is often done alone, but can also be undertaken in a group, which can really help with the empathy parts of group work (see chapter 5). Reflective learning is a way of allowing yourself to step back from your learning experience to develop critical thinking skills and to improve on future performance by analyzing experiences. This helps us to improve our skills and practice, and it isn't as hard as it sounds. Now that we are about halfway through the book, it is time for us to take stock and consider ways of reflecting on what you have already read, but also how integrating reflection into your studies and essays

---

How to cite this book chapter:
Specht, D. 2019. *The Media And Communications Study Skills Student Guide*. Pp. 61–67. London: University of Westminster Press. DOI: https://doi.org/10.16997/book42.f.

will help you be a better student (and sleep better) It is worth keeping in mind the words of English historian Edward Gibbon:

Edward Gibbon

There isn't really a clear and single definition of reflection, but it is about more than just thinking about your studies; the lack of definition, though, makes this chapter tricky, both to read, and to write. We can though talk about some of the benefits of reflection, and give you some pointers about how you might develop your own reflective practice, one that suits you. At its simplest, reflection is thinking for a purpose, in many ways it is like our active listening, but we are listening to ourselves, which most of us are not very good at. Reflection is also about wanting to, or at least being willing to, become a better learner through understanding, and maybe changing, the way we learn. All sounds a bit abstract and difficult at the moment, but we will try some activities to help with this.

This can all be quite a difficult process, as reflection requires us to be critical – although much like when we are engaging with critical reading, we aren't trying to be negative or to think about things in a destructive way, but instead we are engaging in deep questioning and probing about how we learn. And just as with critical reading, it is a really important skill to learn but as we have already seen, most people can't tell you what that means. Luckily this book can – they mean actively challenging both themselves and others… at least they probably do.

We spend most of our lives learning how to learn, although this isn't always something we do consciously. We instead spend a lot of our time thinking about what we have learned, rather than how we learned it. It is important though for us to reflect on the learning process, and think about how we learn individually.

Start by thinking back to an example of studies you have done in the past. For this activity you should think about something where you really felt like you were learning something, or that you were really engaged with. Write down what the subject or theme of the class was, and then make some notes about the way in which you were learning and why you found that class so engaging. This will help you to think about the way in which you learn.

TASK

Topic/Subject/Task: ____

How was I learning?:

Suggesting that you think carefully and reflectively about how you learn, as well as about what you learn, is actually proven through research to help improve your performance (Loo and Thorpe, 2002) – Look at that, research that helps you do your research (cool!). Before we start exploring the process, there are two important things to remember; first there are no guarantees of success here, no one way of learning that will make everything easy, or guarantee high grades, but knowing how you learn is important, and it is likely to be different to those around you, even those on the same course as you. The rest of this book offers a number of templates and cheat sheets, but in this chapter, you will need to develop your own templates. Much like you did in the *planning your time* exercise in chapter 2 – you did do that didn't you? Go on, go and do it now – I can wait.

It is a good idea to start by trying out a few different ways of reflecting on your work and learning, this will help you to find out what works best for you, of course you might want to share ideas, techniques, tips and hints with other students and also try some that seem to work well for them. If they do not work for you though, don't worry, it just means you need something a little different, something just for you!

Now let's think about the whole you (looking back to why you are studying might be helpful here too), two main things will probably affect your approach to learning:

- Your motivation (why did you decide to take this degree?)
- Your previous learning; either at school or on another course, or life experiences.

Ok, now we are going to reflect on some past experiences.

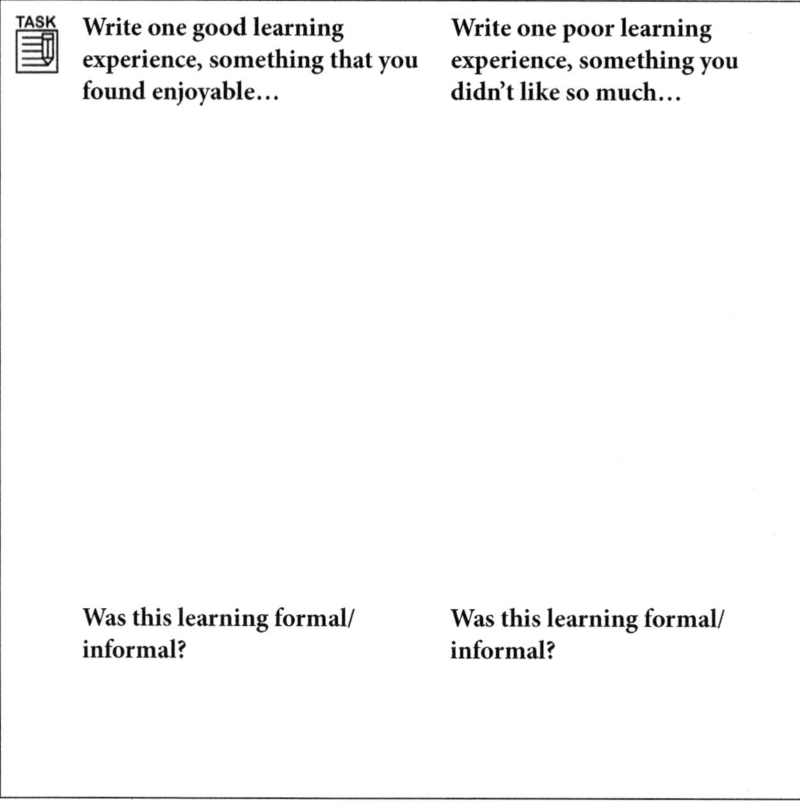

Whatever your answers above, it is likely that you have some emotional relationship to those moments, and about why you wrote them down. We all have a range of positive and negative experiences when it comes to learning, and these are connected to emotion and feelings. When we combine these feelings (or the affective component – to use the clever phrase) with our thinking (the cognitive component) we can become reflective learners, as this enables us to resolve problems and worries about our learning or studies. So, part of the process here is thinking about what parts of your studies make you angry, sad, or happy, and then to think about why that might be the case. Are you angry at your professor because of something they have done, or is it actually a frustration about not understanding the work, or even just the temperature in the room?

When you reflect, you can ask the right questions of your professor about how to improve things – or the caretaker in the case of the temperature. Likewise, don't take for granted the bits you enjoy. Thinking about why you are enjoying them can help you find ways of working independently by creating the same scenarios or environments outside the classroom – although this might be tricky if your favourite thing is a huge room filled with 200 other students, you might upset your housemates in you try to recreate that at home.

TOP TIPS

Reflection as an assessment

Sometimes you will be asked to undertake a reflective exercise as part of an assessment. This might be keeping a diary or a blog that is then seen by your tutor and graded. These kinds of assessments are very useful, but they can leave you feeling exposed as they are asking you to be very personal in your thoughts. While you should be as open and as honest as you can in these tasks, consider also keeping a second notebook to write down those reflections that you feel you don't want to include – often times these are the most important ones for our own development. You can decide later if you want to mention those to your tutor, but the crucial thing is, you have undertaken the personal reflection to help *you*. Don't forget to submit something though!

Other ways to become a reflective learner

We talked about habits and time management in chapter two, and reflective learning has a great deal in common with those points. You're going to do it on some level anyway, so you might as well get used to reflection as part of your everyday learning, and then make it a more active and useful exercise. That way you can use your reflection to help you become a better learner, a better thinker, and maybe even a better person… that last one might be a stretch too far for this book though.

You could record your reflections in a notebook, online in a blog or as an audio file on your phone. You might just jot down a few things at the end of your notes from class (a chance to use another coloured pen). You should though, try and use the reflection process to support your studies, rather than as a separate thing – or something to be avoided. Having already done some reflection is also useful when you go to meetings with your professor, it means you arrive ready to discuss issues or problems you might be facing. But it isn't all negative, thinking about positive experiences you have had can help you to think of strategies that might help you deal with difficult tasks or assignments. This can then all (gradually, it takes time) help you excel as a learning and researcher. Fantastic! We are only halfway through the book and you already excelling!

Before we launch back into writing and research, let's take a moment to recap some key tips. These are the first things we forget when stress hits, so I don't mind repeating myself a little here, because they will help to destress you and help you reflect.

Planning and prioritizing

If you started reading this book at the start of semester one, then you were no doubt wide-eyed and excited about doing your degree perfectly. Like when you start a new notebook, you promise yourself you will do this perfectly, with the best possible handwriting. By now (week 2), you probably feel like you are putting out fires and all your plans have fallen apart. This is quite normal. Your Masters is much more intense than other studies and you may find that you feel a little overwhelmed by your workload and the vast range of different types of activities and skills required by the course.

Figure 6.1: Fine?[4]

But, this is okay! Now you know what is happening and what is expected of you, you can replan and reprioritize your tasks, family, work and hobbies – and luckily you can download as many timetables as you need from our online portal. Draw a new one, that works for the rest of this semester. And don't be

---

[4] This meme from K. C. Green's webcomic *Gumshow* became incredibly popular globally; many academics (probably including some of your tutors) know this feeling and have shared. See https://knowyourmeme.com (2016).

afraid to update it again. Planning is key. One of the ways to keep your motivation up, is to think about why you are here to study, what is it that made you want to start this painful process in the first place? We examined some of that in chapter 2, but you should keep it to the fore of your mind, and you should use it to help you define some more short-term goals. If thinking about your original motivations isn't helping too much, then speak to someone – talk through your motivations and concerns with them, it will help you to find the focus you will need to get through this year.

This will also help with procrastination. We can never fully kill the procrastination monster, but we can tie it down. Reflecting on how, when, where and why you procrastinate can help you to recognize and challenge your routines and habits. So, don't be afraid of making reflection an active part of your day or your week. Doing so helps our brains to file away information and deal with difficult or stressful situations and can also help motivate us and stem procrastination. Reflection can also help us know when things are getting too much before it is too late. And remember your university will have lots of support networks if you are feeling overwhelmed by your studies – don't wait to ask for help in dealing with issues as they arise.

 A study-buddy or peer group can be helpful for working with deadlines. Don't pair up with the perfect student or the waster in the class but someone in the middle like yourself who has good weeks and bad weeks and sometimes needs a reality check or reminder to organise work ahead.

Juan-Pablo– MA student

References

knowyourmeme.com (2016). This is fine. Available at: https://knowyourmeme.com/photos/962640-this-is-fine

Loo, R., & Thorpe, K. (2002). Using reflective learning journals to improve individual and team performance. *Team Performance Management: An International Journal, 8*(5/6), 134–139.

CHAPTER 7

Writing: getting started

Okay. Here we are. Finally. Chapter seven, and we start talking about writing. It's been a long time coming, but I promise you the six chapters before this will make everything much easier. So, if you skipped them, go back and take another look, they are the foundations of good writing. You have been waiting so long for this, so as a reward I am going to pack loads into this chapter, including: planning an essay, structuring your essay, writing your introduction, writing conclusions.

Staring at a blank page, or white screen, is a horrid and daunting prospect, so we are going to break down the process of writing an essay into some steps. The first thing is to make sure you have understood the question (that isn't as easy as you think), then the next thing to do in writing your essay is to state your objective, or thesis. This will tell the reader the viewpoint you are going to express and support in your paper. It will also give you a focus on what you are writing, because the rest of your essay will be to prove the validity of your *thesis statement*. This means a good thesis statement will keep you on topic with your writing, and this will help to focus your reading. Before we get to the rest of the essay, let's look at that more closely.

Understanding the question

It has happened to the best of us, you hand in an essay, quite possibly the best thing you have ever written; maybe even the best thing that has ever been written on the topic. It is full of amazing original ideas, unique insights and could well change the whole world. And then you get your feedback. The mark is low. Red ink (or the digital equivalent) is all over the page; 'not relevant'; 'unrelated'; 'off topic'. Oh no!! What has happened? Then you read to the end of the

How to cite this book chapter:
Specht, D. 2019. *The Media And Communications Study Skills Student Guide*. Pp. 69–88. London: University of Westminster Press. DOI: https://doi.org/10.16997/book42.g. License: CC-BY-NC-ND 4.0

feedback and it says, 'you didn't answer the question'. This is a disaster, and not an uncommon one, but it is also something that can be avoided quite easily by making sure we understand the question we are being asked.

It seems obvious, but ensuring that you are answering the right question is key to gaining the best marks for your work. Many mistakes are made in the understanding of key questioning verbs, and there is nothing more disappointing than pouring your heart and soul into an essay to get feedback that says, 'you didn't answer the question'. So, let's look at the semantics and phrasing of questions. Essay titles include key verbs and words which inform you of how the question must be answered. And if you understand these, then it becomes easy to avoid the scenario above. These key words also provide the framework for your answer and will also help you choose the right essay style. Let's have a look at an example:

'Discuss the relevance of the internet in the analysis of recent social movements in Latin America.'

In this example, there are a number of key words that we need to look out for, the table below breaks this question down:

Discuss	This word instructs you to investigate or examine by argument or debate.
Internet	This is the subject of the question; we need to ensure we understand what is meant by the term internet and need to make this the main focus of the essay.
Recent	Here the question gives us a timeframe. Recent is perhaps a little vague, we might need to consider what the word recent means within the context of other parts of the question.
Social Movements	This is our unit of analysis, or the people/object that we want to study. We must answer the question in relation to social movements.
Latin America	Here we are given the location that we should be focusing on. While other examples might have some relevance, the question should be primarily about Latin America.

As you can see, the question is really guiding the shape of our whole essay and we need to be careful to ensure that we are including all the aspects asked for, while also retaining a focus on those aspects. Perhaps the most important word is the instructional verb at the start of the question (although they can also appear in other places). This tells us the specifics of the shape of our essay. It is really important that you know what each verb means. Some of them have very similar meanings, but your lecturer will have chosen carefully the one in the question, and so you need to be sure to keep them happy by checking what it means. To make this easier, here is a table of the most common instructional verbs that you might come across at university:

Account for	Give reasons for; explain (note: give an account of; describe).
Analyze	Break the information into constituent parts; examine the relationship between the parts; question the information.
Argue	Put the case for or against a view or idea giving evidence for your claims/reasons for or against; attempt to influence the reader to accept your view.
Balance	Look at two or more viewpoints or pieces of information; give each equal attention; look at good and bad points; take into account many aspects and give an appropriate weighting to those aspects.
Be critical	Identify what is good and bad about the information and why; probe, question, identify inaccuracies or shortcomings in the information; estimate the value of the material.
Clarify	Identify the components of an issue/topic/problem; make the meaning plain; remove misunderstandings.
Compare	Look for similarities and differences between; perhaps conclude which is preferable; implies evaluation.
Conclude/draw conclusions	The end point of your critical thinking; what the results of an investigation indicate; arrive at a judgement by reasoning.
Contrast	Bring out the differences.
Criticise	Give your judgement on theories or opinions or facts and back this by discussing evidence or reasoning involved.
Deduce	Conclude; infer.
Define	Give the precise meaning. Examine the different possible or often used definitions.
Demonstrate	Show clearly by giving proof or evidence.
Describe	Give a detailed, full account of the topic.
Determine	Find out something; calculate.
Develop an opinion/ a view	Decide what you think (based on an argument or evidence).
Discuss	Investigate or examine by argument; debate; give reason for and against; examine the implications of the topic.
Elucidate	Explain and make clear.
Estimate	Calculate; judge; predict.
Evaluate/weigh up	Appraise the worth of something in the light of its truth or usefulness; assess and explain.

Examine	Look at carefully; consider.
Explain	Make plain and clear; give reasons for.
Give evidence	Provide evidence from your own work or that of others which could be checked by a third party to prove/ justify what you say.
Identify	Point out and describe.
Identify trends	Identify patterns/changes/ movements in certain directions (e.g. over time or across topics/ subjects).
Illustrate	Explain, clarify, make clear by the use of concrete examples.
Infer	Conclude something from facts or reasoning.
Interpret	Expound the meaning; make clear and explicit, giving your own judgement.
Justify	Show adequate grounds for decisions, a particular view or conclusions and answer main objections likely to be made to them.
Outline	Give a short description of the main points; give the main features or general principles; emphasize the structure, leaving out minor details.
Prove	Show that something is true or certain; provide strong evidence (and examples) for.
Review	Make a survey examining the subject carefully; similar to *summarize and evaluate.*
State	Present in a brief, clear form.
Summarize	Give a concise account of the chief points of a matter, removing unnecessary detail.
Synthesize	Bring elements together to make a complex whole, draw together or integrate issues (e.g. theories or models can be created by synthesizing a number of elements).
Trace	Follow the development of topic from its origin.

Adapted (with thanks) from UELT (2008)

Knowing these verbs is only half the battle, there are some other things we also need to do.

1. Work out exactly what you're being asked

As we said above, you must take time to figure out exactly what you are being asked to do – *what is the question*? Avoid skim-reading and writing the essay you want to write. Instead, identify key words and phrases and write out a plan that covers them all. Don't rush this bit. You can't read the question too many times – oh, well 10,000 might be too many, but you know what I mean.

2. **Be as explicit as possible**
When you start writing use forceful, persuasive language to show how the points you've made *do* answer the question. Use the same terminology and words as the question. Restate the question as *thesis statement* (see below) and use the question to help you shape the concluding paragraph to ensure there is a very explicit answer that a reader can see without even reading the rest of the essay – Do, though be sure the whole essay helps get you to that answer, the conclusion has to match the essay.

3. **Be honest about whether a point is needed**
Sometimes we have some brilliant ideas, or read some amazing quotes, and we really want to get it into our essay, just to show how smart or well-read we are, but if the point isn't actually needed, or relevant to the essay, it can just become a distraction and leave your reader confused about the thread of your argument. Worse, they might miss some of the really good points that you have made. The key is to keep referring back to your plan to *make sure that what you are writing is relevant and answers the question*. When you have finished check the essay again against the question itself. Edit out anything irrelevant and strengthen your main points alongside your *proof reading*.

4. **Choose the right shape for your essay** We will come to that in a moment but first …

Defining a thesis statement

It seems obvious, but every paper you write should have a main point, a main idea, and everything in your essay should link back to this main point. As obvious as this might sound when you're reading this, this is often missing in student essays. To make the main point really clear it should be summarized in one or two sentences called a thesis statement. This statement should let the reader know the topic of your essay and also give your view on the topic, and this will also guide your writing to help you to keep your argument focused. Your thesis statement should come early in your essay – in the introduction, or in longer essays in the second paragraph. It's kind of a spoiler as to what is coming – but unlike *Game of Thrones*, we want to know from the outset your intentions – even if it is to kill all our favourite characters. You should try and be as clear and as specific as possible, but you should avoid boring and cliché sentence structures like, 'The point of my paper is…'. Instead take a look at our examples:

Your idea:

Many people think that modern zombie films are too violent or unpleasant.

Thesis statement:

Modern cinematic techniques mean that films have become more graphic, and this has led to the desensitization of young British filmgoers to violence.

or

The explicit violence in many mainstream zombie movies degrades both men and women.

or

Today's zombie movies fail to deliver the emotional engagement and social subtexts that 1970s zombie films contained.

Thesis statements are *so* important, we are going to spend a bit more time on them. You need to be as clear as you can, so that your reader understands exactly what you mean. You should avoid technical language and jargon – even if you see lots of this in the articles that you are reading (You can be better than them, remember how hard you found these articles to read? Make yours more readable).

You should also avoid vague words such as 'interesting,' 'negative,' 'exciting,' 'unusual,' and 'difficult.' And as with all your writing, don't use what are known as *abstract words* such as 'society,' 'values,' or 'culture.' These words are only useful if you have given a good explanation of that they mean to you and for your essay, you can't assume, for example, that you have the same understanding of what 'society' means as your reader.

You need to be as specific as possible so there can be no misunderstandings. You might have a nice professor who will give you the benefit of the doubt, but they might be having a bad day when marking, so don't risk it – instead, take a look at the examples of how to make a thesis statement clear:

Compare our first attempt at a thesis statement (not specific and clear enough) with the improved version (much more specific and clear):

- **Original thesis statement:** Although Facebook is an enjoyable and fun platform, users are leaving in droves. [if it's so enjoyable and fun, why are people leaving??]
- **Revised thesis statement:** Although Facebook is seen by many as an enjoyable and fun platform, users are leaving in droves over concerns around privacy and data sharing.

TOP TIPS

✓ A thesis statement is about more than just saying, here is my topic! It should also tell the reader what angle you are going to take, or your stance. And should tell the reader why it matters;

- **Original thesis**: In this paper, I will discuss the relationship between fairy tales and modern cinema.
- **Revised thesis**: Not just empty stories for kids, fairy tales can help us understand the modern cinematic experience.

✓ Be careful not to oversimplify complex issues in your thesis statements;

- **Original thesis**: We must save net neutrality.
- **Revised thesis**: Because the internet was designed as an open platform on a basis of equal access and equality, net neutrality is seen as a crucial element of its infrastructure.

✓ If your thesis statement is more subjective (closer to an opinion) then you should give some reasoning for this.

- **Original thesis**: Open Source Software is the best kind for people to use.
- **Revised thesis**: If more software is made open source then developers will be able to more easily build upon ideas and better develop new products and tools.

✓ Don't just state a fact, or something that everyone already knows. Add something new to the debate within your thesis statement:

- **Original thesis**: Facebook was rocked by scandal.
- **Revised thesis**: The many scandals to hit Facebook revealed basic problems with the company's infrastructure and underlying design.

A few final words on thesis statements. Use your own words in thesis statements and avoid quoting. A well-crafted thesis statement reflects well-crafted ideas. It makes the reader believe you are intelligent, committed, and enthusiastic – and you definitely want them to think those things about you. While it's good to start with a reasonably well-formed statement, you will have to come back to this when the essay is finished and edit it a little bit to make sure it really matched what you have said, and the ideas you have. As we are writing our ideas can change, the secret to a good essay is to keep going back over the whole to text to make sure all the ideas still link together – and most important is the thesis statement.

Once you have a good draft thesis statement though, you can begin to map out your essay as a whole.

Preparing a working outline

So, you're read the question, you've done some reading and have a good draft of a thesis statement. It must be time to start writing, surely? Not so fast! One more step before we get into the first full draft. That is to draw up an outline. Many people try and skip this step, but a little thought here can help focus your reading, ensures you have all the information you need for the essay, helps to focus you towards answering the question – and can help you avoid plagiarism – pretty good huh?! They don't sound so bad now do they?

You will first need to decide what type of essay you are going to write, and what shape it will take. The question you have been set will help you do this, but here are some of the most common shapes of essays:

Definition Essay		Classification Essay	
A definition essay involves taking one idea or term and writing about what it is. They require you to give a considered, and clear definition of the term first, before going on to discuss any debates or disagreements in the rest of the essay.		Classification essays are about putting ideas into different categories so you can discuss them one at a time, defining each and then giving examples.	
Example question:	Write an essay defining social media and discuss its different uses.	*Example question:*	Write an essay discussing the three types of software.
Introduction:	Define the key term social media.	*Introduction:*	Give background information about different software standards.
Supporting paragraphs:	1. Define one type of social media: Whatsapp. 2. Define another type of social media: Twitter.	*Supporting paragraphs:*	1. Define and describe open source software. 2. Define and describe freeware. 3. Define and describe closed code software.
Summary paragraph:	Summarize social media.	*Summary paragraph:*	Summarize the whole software landscape.

Description Essay	**Compare and Contrast Essay**
As the name suggests, description essays involve you describing a person, place, thing or concept. You should organize your essay to describe each feature in detail.	In a compare and contrast essay, you write about the similarities and differences between two or more people, places, or things. You can organize the essay by writing about one subject first and then comparing it with the second subject. A more effective way is to organize the essay by comparing each subject by category.

Example question:	Write an essay describing a specific newspaper.	*Example question:*	Write an essay comparing public relations to advertising.
Introduction:	Introduce the newspaper and what a newspaper is.	*Introduction:*	Introduce broad definitions of both PR and advertising.
Supporting paragraphs:	1. Describe where the newspaper is circulated. 2. Describe the politics and dynamics of the newspaper. 3. Describe who reads the newspaper.	*Supporting paragraphs:*	1. Compare the internal operations of PR and of advertising. 2. Compare the outward facing operations of PR to advertising.
Summary paragraph:	Summarize what the newspaper is.	*Summary paragraph:*	Summarize the similarities and differences.

Explanation Essay		Evaluation Essay	
In an explanation essay, you explain how or why something happens or has happened. You need to explain different causes and effects. You should organize the essay by explaining each individual cause or effect.		In an evaluation essay, you make judgments about people, ideas, and possible actions. You make your evaluation based on certain criteria that you develop. Organize the essay by discussing the criteria you used to make your judgment.	
Example question:	Write an essay explaining why newspaper circulation has declined in many Western countries.	*Example question:*	Write an essay evaluating the importance of social media in the Arab Spring.
Introduction:	Give background information on the rates of newspaper circulation.	*Introduction:*	Give your judgment on whether social media was important in the Arab Spring.
Supporting paragraphs:	1. Explain first reason: move to online news sources. 2. Explain second reason: changing printing costs.	*Supporting paragraphs:*	1. Explain first criteria: meeting place for activists. 2. Explain second criteria: activism v. clicktivism. 3. Explain third criteria: surveillance.
Summary paragraph:	Summarize main reasons.	*Summary paragraph:*	Conclude with overall judgement on the role of social media in the Arab Spring.

Once you know the rough shape of your essay start by making a list of the topics you think you will need to include or try creating a mind map such as discussed in notetaking in chapter four. These ideas should come from the reading you have done previously. Once you have that list, divide the ideas or topics on the list into major topics and subtopics following the shape of the essay you have chosen – it might be you decide a different essay shape is needed at this point, and that is okay, just make sure you use a type that helps answer the question. Draw or write these out either on your computer or on paper, but be sure to leave plenty of blank space for your notes. You can now start to sort your notes according to the topics and subtopics in your outline. Once this is done you should have a well-organized plan, with a good structure, all your notes in place and an even better idea of your thesis statement. Don't worry if you need to add more later, this is just the start!

You are now ready to **write the rough draft.** We all like to think we can write perfectly the first time – but we really can't. The important thing in the draft is to get all your ideas down and in the right place, to build the argument, follow your outline and expand your ideas with information from your notes, and don't worry too much at the moment about spelling, punctuation or the formatting of the document – but do make sure you have enough time to come back and fix those things. As the science fiction writer Octavia Butler tells us:

Octavia Butler

When you have finished the rough draft, take a well-deserved break – a walk, sleep, Netflix, anything you like, but step away from the computer, then later come back and read through it again and revise it. When you are reading through your own work, be very careful to look both the content and the overall organisation of the work. Check that every paragraph has a sentence that links it back to your thesis statement. Then check that every paragraph contains some evidence to support that claim, and that it is properly cited. Check that you have made good transitions between paragraphs, and that they build up and argument, rather than feeling like separate ideas – we will cover how to do that in a later chapter. To do a good proofread of a work might require you to read it multiple times, and with different purposes in mind – first for ideas, then for structure, then for spelling for example – so make sure you leave plenty of time for this.

Remember:

Read – Think – Write – Re-write

first	about your ideas	a draft	the essay fixing errors and adding details

TOP TIPS

Use the tools built into Word to help you …

Programs like Word can help you lay out your work and build a structure, this can also become useful later if you need to add a contents page.

1. Add the main section titles to your paper. Select these as header 1 using Word's tools.
2. Add any sub-sections, and make these 'header 2' – it is recommended that you don't use any additional headers.
3. This will allow you to navigate through your document using the navigation pane on the left of the document
4. When you have finished writing, either delete the headings – this should be done on a short essay – or for a longer essay head to the front of the document and insert a table of contents from Word's options. This will automatically pick up all your headings.

Writing introductions

The beginning and end of your essay are the most important parts – obviously the middle is important, too. These are the parts that hook the reader in and then leave them with a sense of your work and definite answer to the essay question. The introduction should be a full paragraph that contains several sentences, beginning with a strong opening statement that makes the reader want to read the whole essay. A few more sentences should continue to draw in the reader and work towards the main point of the work, including a clear thesis statement (see above). There are many different ways we can open an essay, but as they say, first impressions count, so it is well worth considering how you will start. Here are some ideas for different ways to start an essay:

Fact opener

Introductions can grab the reader's attention by starting off with a surprising statement, unusual fact or startling statistic. An essay on the uses of the internet might begin with 'More than three billion people are now regular internet users, yet 10% of households in the United Kingdom do not have any access at all (ONS, 2018)'. Don't forget you must always must always credit the sources of statistics to avoid plagiarism and to maintain credibility.

Quotation opener

Starting an introduction with an insightful quotation relieves you of some of the pressure to be clever (not saying you're not clever, but nice to have a break sometimes). Well-chosen quotations pack a punch, relate clearly to the topic and generally do not exceed two sentences. For example, an essay about algorithms might start. '*Computers will talk to anyone*' stated Sean Cubitt in a recent conference, '*but only the rich teach them to speak*' (*cited in* Summerhayes, 2015); this tells us much of what we need to know about the power of algorithms ...' This hooks the reader in and tells them much of what the essay will be about. You still need a thesis statement though.

Definition opener

Definitions can be a really useful way of starting an essay, especially if you are writing about something controversial or that might not be commonly known about. You should be careful though, a dictionary definition doesn't work well for this; instead you should use a definition from an academic source that defines the term in the way you will use it in your essay. In this way it might be similar to the quote opener. Only use this if your essay requires it. There is no need to define common words, and that would be a weak opening. Yet where the main point of the essay revolves around a word that is ambiguous, then these openings are helpful. You will though still need a thesis statement too!

- ✗ Do not write, 'This essay is about…' or 'In this essay, I will discuss…' instead, just get right into essay using one of our suggested openers above.

- ✗ Do not write a brilliant introduction on the wrong topic. It seems obvious, but we can get caught up in an exciting opening, and then realize it wasn't quite the right topic, so make sure you know what you are writing about before you start writing.

- ✗ Do not use the same opening all the time, it gets boring. Mix it up a bit.

- ✗ Do not get yourself worked up or worried about trying to use the openers here. Trying to force one won't help at all, instead get the essay written, and then come back and make your opening more exciting at the end, this way you will know just what your essay is about.

- ✗ Don't use questions in your opener, or anywhere in your essay for that matter.

The middle

Like a good sandwich, your essay needs to have a good filling, the real meat (or vegetarian option) of your ideas. Your introduction has set the reader up to know what you plan to say. Now you must tell them, and you must convince them. To do this the central part of any essay should contain critical writing. Your professors probably talk about this a lot too, and you have probably had feedback that tells you to be more critical, but what does this really mean? 

Well it is, perhaps unsurprisingly, not dissimilar to critical reading (see how the skills we learn are needed across all aspects, handy that). With critical writing you are telling the reader how much you accept or agree with the things you have read or watched before writing your essay. You are also telling us whether you think the other writers have offered enough evidence for their argument – or to be cleverer, you are evaluating their contribution to the field – fancy!

This is in contrast to descriptive writing, that just describes something. A certain amount of descriptive writing is needed in your essay, particularly in the intro- duction or background, in order to give the setting of the research, to discuss the measurements taken or timing of research in the methodology, or to give biographical details of a key figure or the history leading up to an event or deci- sion. Descriptive writing is easy to do, and you can accidently find yourself using up lots of words from your wordcount by just describing, and at first this might seem like a good idea, as you are asked to write longer and longer essays – but soon you will find comments that tell you to be more critical, and worse, grades that are going down, not up. If you only write descriptions, then you are not enhancing the information, you are just reporting on ideas, but we want to see you advance those ideas through critical writing.

Writing critically means that you are becoming part of the academic debate (ooow, fancy!). This though, is more challenging and risky (boo!). To do criti- cal writing you need to be able to weigh up the quality of evidence and work presented by others, and to consider carefully how convincing you find the information in front of you. You need to make notes of the positive and nega- tive parts of the argument, and also to think about which parts are relevant to your essay (either in support, or to show the other side of the debate). These ideas then need to be synthesized together (see chapter 8). All this takes a great deal more brain power, but it is the way to access the highest marks, and to avoid the 'be more critical' comment from your professor.

Let's now look now in more detail about how to do critical writing, paragraph by paragraph. Rather than just filling our essay with quotes, we want to work to build arguments and ideas using our own words. The best way to do this is to think about each paragraph as a miniature essay. Each paragraph is made up of four parts:

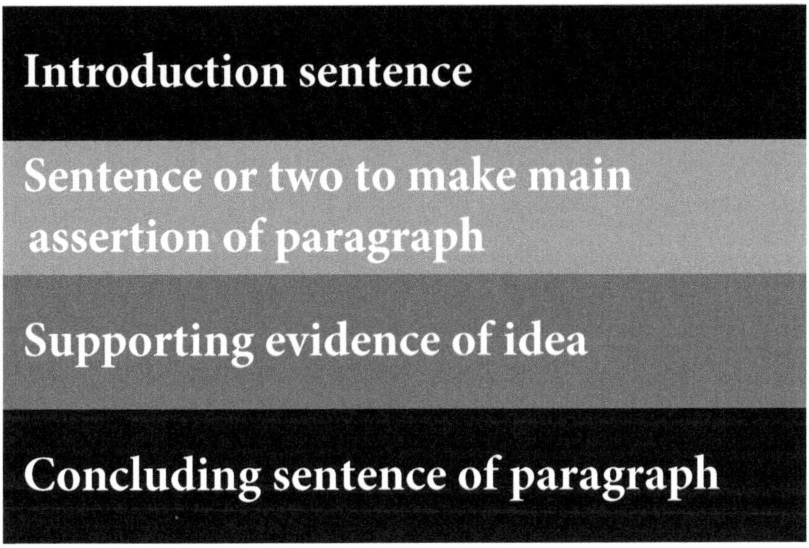

Introduction sentence

Sentence or two to make main assertion of paragraph

Supporting evidence of idea

Concluding sentence of paragraph

Figure 7.1: Paragraph structure.

Just like with your essay as a whole, the opening of a paragraph should, in one sentence, tell is what is about to happen, the main argument of the paragraph. This should be followed with a couple of sentences about why you make that assertion – with some references to the ideas you have used. Then give the reader some evidence, again this will be a thought or data from someone else's work, so make sure you reference it well. Finally, show the reader how the idea links to the main (thesis statement) of your essay, before linking this paragraph to the next one. You need to make each paragraph convincing to the reader, and the best way to do this is to reference your sources.

Even with excellent paragraphs, it is also important to consider the overall structure of your piece of writing. You should make sure that everything leads back to answering the question, but also that the whole essay has a logic. Using the essay shapes provided will help you with this too, but when you finish the essay you should also read it from beginning to end to make sure your argument and thoughts didn't get lost along the way, and that your readers will be able to follow what you are thinking.

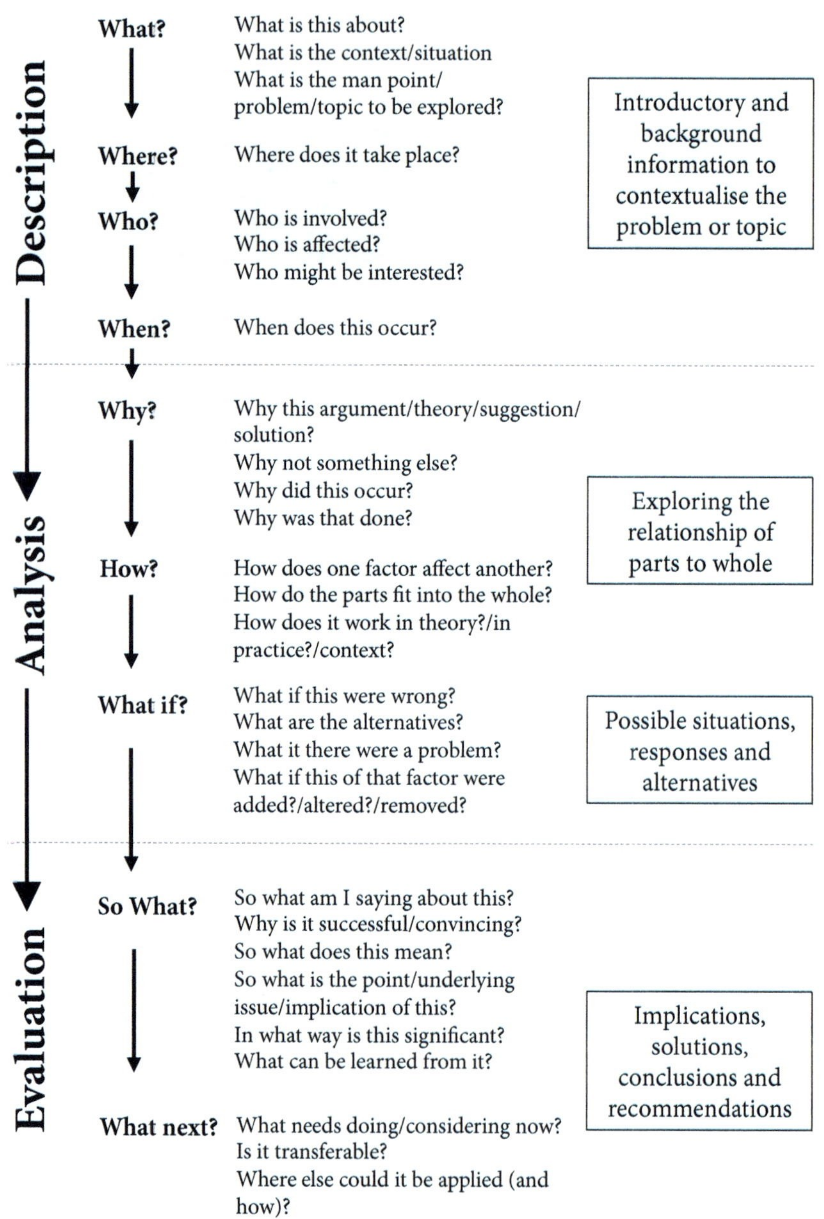

Figure 7.2: From description to evaluation; from Hilsden (2010).

Example of critical writing:

There are of course a wide range of perspectives about what technology is and its relation to society (Hutchby, 2001), what is of great concern though is the ease with which links are made both between the function of technology in producing poverty and de-worlding effects (Feenberg, 2005), and conversely its ability to solve issues of poverty through the production and analysis of data which can enable better targeting of poverty reduction schemes (Taylor and Broeders, 2015). In the last decade, these technologies have become increasingly prolific in nature and have been further and further integrated into the work of NGOs, development organizations and embodied within poor societies (Atzmanstorfer *et al.*, 2014). There is already a contradiction here, as some of the largest technology companies, and philanthropists engage in the fight against poverty, they are also pushing for the liberalization of public services and the virtues of neoliberalism (Zamora, 2014). Technologies corresponding to different civilizations have always co-existed (Feenberg, 1991), but as the juggernaut of neoliberal digital tools spreads across the world and the development sector, questions around what counts as data, and whose data counts are becoming increasingly urgent (Burns, 2015).

Authors own, in-text citations in references at end of chapter.

Writing conclusions

Generally speaking, conclusion paragraphs are about 5% of your essay word count and they should serve to 'round-off' the essay, remind the reader of the key points and to give an answer to the question posed. You should restate the thesis from your introduction (without repeating it word for word), make a brief summary of your evidence and finish with some sort of judgment about the topic. (See figure 7.3).

It's a good idea to start your conclusion with transitional words (words like 'In summary', 'To conclude', 'In conclusion', 'Finally',) as these help the reader to know that you about to give them your killer final point and they should wake up. We don't add new ideas in the conclusion, so conclusions don't usually have many citations, apart from maybe a great quote from someone special as a final word. The conclusion to an essay is rather like a formal social farewell, and you want to leave the party (I mean essay) in a dignified manner – Not in a horrible mess, unsure of what happened and not knowing why your significant other isn't talking to you. Okay, that last part is just about parties, but with your essay,

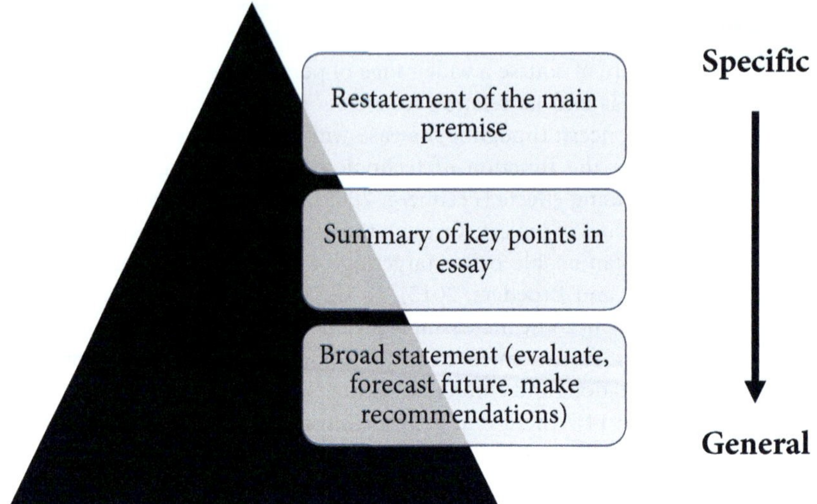

Figure 7.3: Conclusions.

you also don't want to leave things a mess. So, make it clear how they end – the essay, not the relationship with your significant other.

TOP TIPS

FINDING YOUR ACADEMIC VOICE

When you engage in critical writing you are developing your own academic voice within your subject. Wellington *et al.* (2005 p.84) offer some suggestions for distinguishing between the academic and the non-academic voice. They suggest that the academic voice will involve:

- ✓ healthy skepticism … but not cynicism;
- ✓ confidence … but not 'cockiness' or arrogance;
- ✓ judgement which is critical … but not dismissive;
- ✓ opinions … without being opinionated;
- ✓ careful evaluation of published work … not serial shooting at random targets;
- ✓ being 'fair': assessing fairly the strengths and weaknesses of other people's ideas and writing … without prejudice; and
- ✓ 'making judgements on the basis of considerable thought and all the available evidence … as opposed to assertions without reason.'

(Wellington *et al.*, 2005)

Phew! That is a lot to get your head around. I would suggest reading through this section again before every essay, and then taking it one step at a time. Remember you need to know what the question is before you can start, then read around that topic for a while before drafting a thesis statement. You can then make a plan before doing targeted reading, and follow this up by arranging your notes into sections. Later we will look at some more advanced writing techniques, but remember all academic writing follows the same formula, so use the models in this chapter. Even your professors use these models, but they hold them in their head because they have been doing this (in some cases much) longer than you. Let's now move towards really advancing our skills through combining sources … onwards to chapter 8!

A note on audio/visual assessments

Being a cool media and communications student, you might be asked to present your essay work in the form of a video, podcast or even a radio programme. While there will be specific instructions from your tutors about what they want, all the principles laid out above (and below actually) will also still count. You will still need to define the thesis, the main point of argument. You will still need to plan the shape of your argument, and the essay shapes can be adapted to audio or visual essays too. You still need to have good conclusions and a strong introduction. It is easy to get overexcited about the production of an audio/visual essay, so make sure you keep our essay principles in mind, even when the form of assessment is more exciting.

References

Atzmanstorfer, K., Resl, R., Eitzinger, A., & Izurieta, X. (2014). The GeoCitizen-approach: community-based spatial planning–an Ecuadorian case study. *Cartography and geographic information science, 41*(3), 248–259.

Burns, R. (2015). Rethinking big data in digital humanitarianism: Practices, epistemologies, and social relations. *GeoJournal, 80*(4), 477–490.

Feenberg, A. (1991). *Critical theory of technology*. New York: Oxford University Press.

Feenburg, A. (2005). Critical theory of technology: An overview. *Tailoring biotechnologies*. Vol 1(1) p. 47–64.

Hilsden, J. (2010). 'Critical Thinking', Learning Development, Available from: https://www.plymouth.ac.uk/uploads/production/document/path/1/1713/Model_To_Generate_Critical_Thinking.pdf (Accessed: March 2019)

Hutchby, I. (2001). Technologies, texts and affordances. *Sociology, 35*(2), 441–456.

Summerhayes, C. (2015). *Google Earth: Outreach and activism.* Bloomsbury Publishing USA.

Taylor, L. & Broeders, D. (2015). In the name of development: Power, profit and the datafication of the global South. *Geoforum, 64,* 229–237.

UELT (2008). Instruction verbs in essay questions. The Unit for the Enhancement of Learning and Teaching [Online] Available from: https://www.kent.ac.uk/ai/ask/documents/step_1_Instruction_verbs.pdf Accessed March 2019.

Wellington, J., Bathmaker, A., Hunt, C., McCulloch, G. & Sikes, P. (2005). *Succeeding with your doctorate.* London: Sage.

Zamora, D. (2014). Can We Criticize Foucault? Jacobin [Online] Available from: https://www.jacobinmag.com/2014/12/foucault-interview/ Accessed Oct 2015.

CHAPTER 8

Reading and notetaking: combining sources

Haven't we done this already? Well, yes, we looked at ways of taking notes in chapter 4, but now let's do some advanced notetaking that will allow us to write in a really high-quality academic style. We are going to look further at ways of reading, how to combine information and how to synthesize reading to create complex and interesting essays that will blow your professors socks off. And the best thing is, this is all easier than you might think – especially with a bit of practice.

There are just six steps for reading in this way;

❏ Previewing
❏ Annotating
❏ Outline, summarize, analyze
❏ Look for repetitions and patterns
❏ Contextualize
❏ Compare and contrast.

Many of these are skills that will already seem familiar from earlier chapters, but here we are going to step things up to a new level. You are about to become an expert reader and note-taker! So, let's take a look at each of these a little closer.

How to cite this book chapter:
Specht, D. 2019. *The Media And Communications Study Skills Student Guide*. Pp. 89–100.
    London: University of Westminster Press. DOI: https://doi.org/10.16997/book42.h.
    License: CC-BY-NC-ND 4.0

WILLIAM E. B. DU BOIS

1. Previewing

This is something we covered pretty well in chapter 4, but since it is so important, I'm going to repeat myself a little (not sorry). Before you even begin reading take a look at the basic information about the paper, ask yourself lots of questions – you might want to write them out at first, but soon they will become second nature in your head – and you will ask them about everything you read for the rest of your life, there is no escape once you have become a true critical reader! What does the abstract tell you? Is the author already known to you? If so, how does their reputation influence your thoughts about what you are going to read? What type of article do you have? Is it peer reviewed – that is one that other researchers have said is of academic quality – or is it a press article or something online? Is the material broken into parts, subtopics, sections? Another important area to consider is the date of publication, what was happening in the world that year that might change the way you read the article. For example, what technology was available, what was the political climate? – An article published before 1990 might be tied up in Cold War thinking. Or a piece about the internet published before 2004 won't have heard of Facebook.

2. Annotate

Now we get to more in-depth versions of what we were doing in chapter 4, where I told you about how to read with a highlighter. Well, perhaps that wasn't wise, because really, they are a short-cut to good reading, it is better to throw away your highlighter! (sorry about that). Highlighters can actually distract you from the learning. Those bright yellow lines you put on a page one day can become meaningless the next day, and remember, we are all bad at remembering. Using a pen or pencil, rather than a highlighter, will allow you do to more to a text. You can highlight key things, but still use the margins to make notes of ideas and thoughts, and to make links to class discussion, other texts or your essay topic. Doing it this way helps keep you awake, helps you to stay focused on why you are reading. And then later when you come to look back at your readings it helps avoid those 'what was that?' moments – Remember though, don't annotate the library books, instead photocopy pages or buy your own before writing notes on the page. Your notes won't help others, even if they are fantastic.

3. Outline, summarize, and analyze

Those notes in step two are all well and good, but the only way to know that you really understand a text is to be able to put it in your own words. You need to pull the text apart, and then rebuild it in your own words. This doesn't have to be too formal to start with. Outlining an article which you are reading is like doing the opposite of an essay plan – you

are looking for the skeleton of the article. You should make clear notes about its thesis statement. Each point of evidence. And what its conclusions might be. Not all writers are as good as you, so it might take some hunting, but all this information is in there.

Summarizing is very similar to outlining, but now we use full sentences and paragraphs to achieve this. It is though still for your eyes only (very James Bond), and won't be appearing in an essay without a lot of editing. To really get good at reading and notetaking, and of course that is what we are aiming at, we need to add analysis – another word you hear a lot, but it isn't always clear what it means. Analyzing adds evaluation, it means not just restating the main ideas, but also testing them against other ideas. When analyzing a text, you decide how well (or badly) its argument has been presented by the author. You should look at the evidence that the author supplies to try and convince you, and then look for places where that evidence isn't strong enough or isn't well supported.

If you can see these strengths and weaknesses, then congratulations! You are now well on your way to becoming a great critical thinker and writer – but there are a couple more things to think about.

4. Look for repetitions and patterns

This can be an easy one. We all have that friend who keeps repeating a joke or comment until everyone acknowledges then, well writers can do

MICHEL FOUCAULT

the same. Look at the way language is chosen, positioned and repeated, this can tell you a lot about what an author thinks is most important, and it can also suggest to you their ideological position, their hidden agendas or their biases. When you see repeated words, phrases, types of examples do make a note of them, this will help you to better summarize the author's work.

5. Contextualize

Phew! We are getting there with our advanced reading techniques, but we are still not quite ready to use these notes for writing. Once you've finished reading and annotating, try thinking about the text from other perspectives. There is more on this in chapter 4, but simply when you contextualize, you essentially look at the text again (yes, again!) and consider how it might be shaped by historical, cultural, material, or intellectual circumstances – this is clearly linked to step one, but now you have read the text fully. Do these factors change, complicate, explain, deepen or otherwise influence how you view a piece? This is also related to noting the date of the text, and the type of publication. Also examine the reading through your own experience. Your life and past experiences will have a big influence on how you understand the text, or how much you like it, and while few essays ask you for your own opinion, thinking about the text this way will help highlight your own biases and prejudices as you begin writing. As we will see in chapter 9, this is very important even if we don't get to write about it, as philosopher and cultural critic Walter Benjamin said.

WALTER BENJAMIN

6. Compare and contrast

Finally, the last step, then we can do some seriously good writing. Once you have read a few different texts you need to see if you can find any relationships. Which of the texts share ideas? Which ones oppose each other? What are the general themes? If you are looking at texts your professor has given you, how does the order you were asked to read them change your thinking? They will almost certainly have a plan in mind when they choose the order of your readings – can you work it out? How has your thinking been altered by this reading, or how has it affected your response to the issues? Again, make sure you make some good and clear notes here. It doesn't matter which method of notetaking you use, and they don't have to be really long, but to write a good essay you must start noting how things fit together – and that also makes the next step much much easier!

TOP TIPS

Annotated bibliographies

Sometimes you might be asked to combine these skills to make an annotated bibliography (or you might think it is useful for yourself). In an annotated bibliography we make a list of the references for each thing we have read, and under that we write about 250–300 words that discuss that text. We would use that short paragraph to talk about all those things listed above; an outline, context, patterns, credentials of the author, comparisons, and so forth. These can make really useful notes for writing an essay.

Turning notes into essays: summarizing, paraphrasing, and synthesizing

The time has come! The preparation is done, your notes are made. Go and make a large cup of tea. Turn off (or turn on if you prefer) the radio. We are going to start writing. This is the fun bit, the creative bit, you're like the Hannah Höch of writing, a collagist bringing ideas together from everywhere to create a new masterpiece! But hang on, many students still find this process of incorporating other sources or 'voices' into their writing difficult, but this is what we need to do. Your professor wants to see a range of sources to support your views and ideas.

So, before you start, look back at chapter 4 at the two main ways you can include someone else's ideas into your work using proper citations – those are of course direct quotation (transferring exact words) and indirect reporting (such as paraphrases and summaries). As we said before, you should always be looking for a combination of these types, along with some of your own voice (see chapter 9 for more on that). And provided you have been taking good notes while reading, then the next stages of using these quotes and indirect reporting will be much easier. The first step is to look back at those notes and texts and decide in which way we will include information from them in our essay. There are three basic ways to do this:

• Summarize • Paraphrase • Synthesize

Summarizing

A summary is a shortened version of the original text. It should contain the main points of the original text but in a condensed version. It should be written in your own words. The source should, of course, be acknowledged. A summary should start with a clear opening about the type of work, title, author, and main point of the article and this should be in the present tense. You should not put any of your own ideas, opinions, or interpretations into the summary (sorry, we aren't interested in them here). In a summary we only care about what the text says.

You've already noted the key points, so now, while it might seem unfair on the writer of the text, you should delete most details, examples and unimportant information. You should keep any specialist vocabulary, but you can change the structure of the text. Changing adjectives to adverbs to nouns to verbs, make longer sentences shorter and shorter sentences longer (you're an academic DJ). Use conjunctions and adverbs (see later in this chapter) to join your ideas together combining paragraphs to make a continuous piece of writing. To do a good summary you need to make sure you understand the original text. This also includes considering your purpose for using this text. Ask why you are using it. Is it to support your point or to criticize the text before?

Look at journal articles that have provided good summaries. These can help you to learn the skill of summarizing. The example below is a good place to get started:

Emmers-Sommer, T. M., & Allen, M. (1999). Surveying the effect of media effects: A meta-analytic summary of the media effects research in Human Communication Research. *Human Communication Research*, 25(4), 478–497.

Paraphrasing

Sometimes you may want to be a little more true to the text you have read, but you don't want to use a quote (remember those should be kept to a minimum). To do this we can use paraphrasing. You should limit paraphrasing to short bits of text – too much of it and your work won't look like your own. You still need to change the words and the structure of the original, but this time you keep the meaning much closer to the original. And, of course you still need to reference the work (obviously). Paraphrasing is really useful for helping you to clarify or restate an idea, and is essential for good academic writing, but be warned unsuccessful paraphrasing can end up looking like plagiarism, even if you didn't do that on purpose (EEK!). Take a look at our things to avoid below to help with this;

When paraphrasing, there are a few common mistakes you should learn to avoid:

× Don't just swap words or the order of sentences, you need to rewrite the work in your own words completely (although keep specialist language).

× Don't forget to put a full in-text citation for the work or works you have taken the ideas from.

× Don't forget to include quotation marks around any terms or phrasing that you have borrowed from the author, and then add the page number of where this quote came from.

Synthesizing

Summarizing and paraphrasing are very useful tools, but to really write a fantastic piece of work we need to look at synthesizing. This is when you combine several texts into one, usually shorter, piece of writing. Synthesizing is an important, but complex skill required in academic writing. It involves combining ideas from a range of sources in order to group and present common ideas or arguments, it also cites multiple sources. There are two main ways of synthesizing, bringing together similar ideas, and bringing together contrasting ideas. This is where you become a fantastic writer – it really doesn't get any better than this!

Synthesizing a similar idea:

Once you have done sufficient readings (how many is that I hear you ask – well it's enough when you start to see patterns emerging in the opinions and ideas of authors). You will see that there are many authors who say similar things, but it becomes rather boring for the reader if we just keep listing authors and stating that they say the same thing, and you don't want to be accused of being boring. So, instead we can use some shortcut and clever writing to be able to bring those ideas together into a succinct and solid sentence or paragraph.

In this example, we have read three texts, all of which discuss the way in which social media has been used in protests as a useful tool. In our notetaking we have put these texts all together as sharing an idea and now we want to tell our readers about these ideas by synthesizing them into a short sentence:

Notes from reading

Synthesized text in essay

Synthesizing contrasting ideas

Now we are going to write a more complex pair of sentences that contrast two sets of readings. From our notes we can see that we have two texts that believe that social media is useful for protest movements, and two that say that it is not so useful, or even problematic. See how the sythnesiszed text reflects these two different opinions:

Notes from reading

Texts that say social media is useful

Text 1
Shirky (2011)

Text 2
Jost *et. al.* (2018)

Texts that say social media is NOT useful

Text 3
Cook *et. al.* (2014)

Text 4
Trottier and Fuchs (2014)

Synthesized text in essay

Supporting the contention that social media are able to support protest movements, Shirky (2011) and Jost *et. al.* (2018) pointed out its importance as the medium of communication across disparate social movements. However, others argue that despite its apparent usefulness, issues of surveillance and slacktivism can actually mean that social media hinders protest movements (Cook *et. al.*, 2014; Trottier and Fuchs, 2014).

Now, let's look at one last example where we pull together all our notetaking, summarizing, paraphrasing and synthesizing to create a complex paragraph. First, we need to look at the notes that have been made in preparation for this piece of writing:

Source	Main Idea	Quote	Page
Orwell, 1945	Language can corrupt thought.	But if thought corrupts language, language can also corrupt thought. A bad usage can spread by tradition and imitation, even among people who should and do know better.	16
Koskela, 2012	Appearance and reality are the same.	For Heidegger, how a thing appears and the thing itself are interconnected for him and in many ways they are the same.	117
Lyon, 2015	Everyone is a victim of surveillance.	Snowden's work shows that everyone is susceptible to surveillance and anyone's life can unravel due to surveillance 'mistakes' and inadequacies.	139
Marx, 2016	Academics don't give solid answers.	Academics get splinters from fence sitting as a result of their culture or personality.	303
Dwyer, 2016	Our writing can make our fear about surveillance worse.	My intention has not been to generate more fear and panic over the changing conditions of personal privacy. On the contrary I have wanted to critically reflect on these broader transformations in media industries and media consumption practices.	182

Notes taken using a liner method

Now, take a look how these ideas have been used in the following paragraph:

Orwell was useful to Packard, he conjured up the perfect image of the duality between the watched and the watcher, but in a liquid surveillance world (**Lyon, 2010**) another of his texts becomes more useful; *Politics and the English Language*. Here **Orwell (1945)** writes, 'that if thought corrupts language, language can also corrupt thought. A bad usage can spread by tradition and imitation, even among people who should know better' (16). We could take this further, evoking Heidegger, it is the assertions about entities in the world that makes the relationship between them (**Koskela, 2012**); the appearance of a thing, and the thing itself are interconnected, they are one and the same (*ibid.*). Yet, in writings on surveillance and privacy, it is often noted, even by the authors themselves (**Dwyer, 2016; Marx, 2016; Lyon 2015**), that the writing itself may well be creating the same fears and impotence that is ruinous to democracy.

(Specht, 2017)

Being able to synthezise is key to doing really good academic writing. It is a skill that takes practice and sometimes going through the step-by-step process can feel like it is really slowing down your writing. You will get quicker at these skills, but at first it is really important to leave enough time for your essay to ensure you can get through all the steps before you begin writing fully. As you get more practisced these skills will start to become second nature. Having said that, all academic writers still go through these steps when working on their texts. This includes your professors and tutors and all the other writers of texts that you read.

The only way to get your writing as good as theirs is to give yourself time to use the same techniques as them, which means working hard to engage with critical reading, building on chapter 4 and then using the skills in this chapter to push things further. Then use the essay shapes and paragraph models and some synthesizing to really get your work to the highest levels.

References

Cook, D.M., Waugh, B., Abdipanah, M., Hashemi, O., & Rahman, S.A. (2014). Twitter deception and influence: Issues of identity, slacktivism, and puppetry. *Journal of information warfare, 13*(1), 58–71.

Dwyer, T. (2016). *Convergent media and privacy*. Basingstoke and New York: Palgrave Macmillan.

Foucault, M. (2013). *The archaeology of knowledge*. Oxon: Routledge.

Jost, J.T., Barberá, P., Bonneau, R. *et al.* (2018). How social media facilitates political protest: Information, motivation, and social networks. *Political psychology, 39*, 85–118.

Koskela, J. (2012). Truth as unconcealment in Heidegger's *Being and Time*: *Minerva-an Internet journal of philosophy,* 16: 116–128

Lyon, D. (2010). Liquid surveillance: The contribution of Zygmunt Bauman to surveillance studies. *International political sociology, 4*(4): 325–338

Lyon, D. (2015). *Surveillance after Snowden*. Malden: Polity

Marx, G.T. (2016). *Windows into the soul: Surveillance and society in an age of high technology*. Chicago: University of Chicago Press.

Orwell, G. (1945) [2013]. 'Politics and the English Language' In *68*, New York.

Shirky, C. (2011). The political power of social media: Technology, the public sphere, and political change. *Foreign affairs*, 28–41.

Skoric, M.M., Poor, N.D., Liao, Y. & Tang, S.W.H. (2011, January). Online organization of an offline protest: From social to traditional media and back. In *2011 44th Hawaii international conference on system sciences* (pp. 1–8). IEEE.

Specht, D. (2017). Undressing with the lights on: Surveillance and *The Naked Society* in a digital era. *Westminster papers in communication and culture*. 12(3): pp.78–90.

Trottier, D. and Fuchs, C. (Eds.). (2014). *Social media, politics and the state: Protests, revolutions, riots, crime and policing in the age of Facebook, Twitter and YouTube*. Routledge.

CHAPTER 9

The 'I' in academic writing

'I' – some people hate this word in academic writing – some people don't mind it at all. But this very short word can get you into all kinds of trouble in your essays. How can such a small thing cause so many issues? Well, academic writing seeks to reach objectivity. And in your essays your tutors often want to hear more about what you have read, rather than what you think. The problem is, they *do* want to know what you think, but sentences like 'I think…' are over simplistic, and so professors often ban the word 'I' 'and tell you to write only in the third person. They do this to help you build an academic writing style more easily, but it can mean you go missing from your work, so this chapter explores how to position yourself within your writing without using the dreaded 'I' word.

This chapter will examine using attributive verbs and hedging to create a sense of objectivity that allows you to seem less biased and, therefore, more credible – a key part of academic writing. It should be noted though, that not all writing needs to follow these principles, when working on reflective journals, or being asked specifically to express your opinions or to explore your own relationship to a piece of work, it is essential to write 'I' and use the first person. Most people find writing in the first person easier, which is why this chapter is going to concentrate on how to write in the third person, that way you're covered whatever the task.

The easiest way for us to explain this is to look at some examples, look at the difference between the two sentences below.

First person	Third person
Even though Smith thinks this way, *I* think his argument is incorrect.	Even though Smith thinks this way, *others* in the field disagree.

How to cite this book chapter:

Specht, D. 2019. *The Media And Communications Study Skills Student Guide*. Pp. 101–107. London: University of Westminster Press. DOI: https://doi.org/10.16997/book42.i. License: CC-BY-NC-ND 4.0

It is clear that the second sentence is more objective, and even if that isn't clear, trust me, it sounds much more traditionally academic than the first. Just writing in the third person though doesn't quite do everything we need. The third person makes us look objective, even when we are not. Instead we need to be clearer, and write both in the third person *AND* show our opinion. While this sounds hard, it is actually really exciting and this is where your writing starts to get really good. An important part of synthesizing text is deciding how much you agree (or disagree) with the claims other authors make. You need to show that position, even as you quote, summarize, or paraphrase your sources, as this will position you in the ongoing conversation.

To avoid adding an 'I think … ' sentence, we use **attributive verbs** (oow, fancy!) These are special words that show how much you agree or disagree with an idea. And they are not as hard to use as you think. In fact, you probably use them every day, but they do need some care and thought when you are using them in your writing.

Not everybody likes attributive verbs, Elmore Leonard (2010), an American novelist, who thought they were a real problem in writing novels once said, '[n]ever use a verb other than 'said' to carry dialogue. The line of dialogue belongs to the character; the verb is the writer sticking his [or her] nose in'.

This might be good advice for novelists, but it isn't very good advice for academics (we are into chapter 9 now, so you get to call yourself one of those). Leonard thought that the writer shouldn't try and influence the way a reader thought about the quote (he thought that was the author having too much influence), but in academic writing you need to do the opposite, you need to tell the reader just what you think about the quote through the use of attributive verbs. Why? Well because an academic essay is you adding to an ongoing conversation on your topic, and so we want to hear your voice. The word 'said' isn't helpful for us.

Attributive verbs at their simplest, signal that you, the writer, is quoting, paraphrasing, or referring to another source – something we must always do, as you know by now. 'Says' is the most common – and boring – attributive verb, but there are so many that we could use and they all have a special meaning and a special weight to them, meaning they show what you are thinking without you writing 'I think…'. Before we look at all of them, let's look at some simple examples of how they can change the meaning of a sentence. For instance, let's think about the differences between the following sentences:

> Jones (2012) **<u>said</u>** that social media is damaging for children.
> Jones (2012) **<u>shows</u>** that social media is damaging for children.
> Jones (2012) **<u>suggests</u>** that social media is damaging for children.

All three of these sentences would be acceptable ways to introduce Jones' ideas, and they are cited correctly too (well done!). The first though is very dull, and very neutral, it shows nothing of what you think about Jones' idea (Elmore would love it, but we don't). The second example is much stronger, here the reader will think that you find Jones' argument persuasive. Writing that someone **shows** something tells your reader that you think that the claim or idea is correct and that there is enough evidence to support it (see how clever these words are?). **Suggests** on the other hand gives you a way out, it tells the reader that you think the claim or idea might be wrong – careful though, because you aren't saying it *is* wrong, just that it is still open to debate. If you wanted to distance yourself even further, while again not specifically saying the writer is wrong, you could write 'Jones **seems to think** that social media is damaging for children'. Wow! Aren't these words great!

Here are some more examples:

Jones (2012) <u>asserts</u> that social media is damaging for children. That is, he makes a forceful statement but may not offer evidence to support it (or at least you don't find the evidence persuasive).

Jones (2012) <u>concludes</u> that social media is damaging for children.
Here we are saying that Jones has offered up a lot of clear evidence to reach a conclusion – again you don't have to agree, but you are acknowledging the evidence base.

Jones (2012) <u>points out</u> that social media is damaging for children.
In this case, you are suggesting that you think what Jones is saying is correct, and you are also expecting that your readers will agree.

There are so many exciting attributive verbs that you could use, but it is really important that you know what they mean, as they will be telling your readers what you think of the ideas. Use this table, adapted from Centralia (n.d.), to help you:

General attributive verbs:

Accepts	Decides	Offers
Acknowledges	Declares	Points out
Addresses	Defends	Proposes
Adds	Defines	Questions
Advises	Describes	Realizes
Allows	Discusses	Reasons
Analyzes	Echoes	Relates
Answers	Emphasizes	Remarks
Asks	Exclaims	Replies
Asserts	Explains	Reports
Assumes	Expresses	Responds
Assures	Finds	Reveals
Argues	Grants	Sees
Believes	Holds	Speculates
Categorizes	Hypothesizes	States
Challenges	Illustrates	Suggests
Charges	Implies	Supposes
Cites	Indicates	Thinks
Claims	Insists	Uses
Comments	Interprets	Utilizes
Compares	Introduces	Warns
Concedes	Lists	Wonders
Concludes	Maintains	Writes
Considers	Mentions	
Contends	Notes	
Deals with	Observes	

Showing agreement:

Affirms	Concurs with	Supports
Agrees	Confirms	Verifies
Concedes	Echoes	

<table>
<tr><td colspan="3">Showing disagreement:</td></tr>
<tr><td>Condemns</td><td>Derides</td><td>Opposes</td></tr>
<tr><td>Counters</td><td>Disagrees</td><td>Refutes</td></tr>
<tr><td>Criticizes</td><td>Disputes</td><td>Rejects</td></tr>
<tr><td>Denies</td><td>Objects</td><td></td></tr>
</table>

Adapted from Centralia (n.d.).

Attributive verbs are one of your most powerful tools in positioning yourself in your research, and in case you haven't guessed yet, one of my favourite parts of the English language and academic writing. But you must be careful! These words are fantastic because they all have very specific meanings, however that can also get you into trouble if you are not sure what those meanings are. If you aren't sure then use a dictionary to check before you use the word. Also be aware that some verbs require special sentence structures – sadly it isn't possible to just swap 'says' for all of the words above, for example, the verb 'accounts for' must be followed by a noun. And we haven't even looked at all the words, there are actually more than 300 attributive verbs in English (wow!). So, there are plenty of exciting ways to introduce ideas in your work, but you have to select the right one to show your thoughts about the texts you have read. These verbs are your best friend in showing your opinion in your essays without getting told off for bringing non-academic sentences that start 'I think...' into your work.

Hedging your bets

Another good way to show your thoughts and opinions is to use what is called *hedging* to show how much you agree with an idea you are writing about. A hedge can change very forceful statements into much softer ones, and shows you are aware that there are other ideas and opinions out there. So, you can change words from *will*, to *may* or *might*. Or you could write *some* instead of *all*. Or even include an extra word where there wasn't one before. Compare these two sentences:

- Social media triggers mental health issues.
- Social media *may* trigger mental health issues.

The first sentence suggests high level of certainty, it is presented as a fact. The second sentence, is more tentative, meaning you are less sure, suggesting that mental health issues will occur only in certain circumstances or under certain conditions, but not necessarily all the time. The first statement would also be difficult to defend, but the second could be argued more easily.

Hedging then allows us to make claims based on how much evidence we actually have, and you will know how much evidence there is because of your notetaking. So if there is a lot of evidence for something, then we can use strong language to show that, but if something is less sure, or doesn't happen all the time, then we can hedge the language to show that is the case, and this helps to avoid, or at least reduce, criticism of your work. As with the attributive verbs though, there are huge numbers of words and phrases we can choose from, and it is important to choose one that accurately represents what you are trying to say.

Let's look at a few examples, the use of the word 'probably' in the sentence below indicates that the evidence is fairly strong. In the second sentence, the more tentative word 'could' was selected, indicating that the evidence is weak.

- The traditional newspaper's demise was **probably** caused by increases in online news sources.
- The demise of traditional newspapers **could** have been caused by increases in online news sources.

Hedging can also be used when an idea has been later changed or refuted;

- Johnson (2007) **appears to** ignore the adverse psychological side-effects selfie culture.
- The role of social media in protests **may** have been overstated.

<table>
<tr><td colspan="3">A wide range of words and phrases can be used in hedging:</td></tr>
<tr><td>

Modal auxiliary verbs:
can, could, may, might, should, would</td><td>

Other modal verbs:
appear, look, seem, tend</td><td>

Probability adjectives:
likely, possible, probable, unlikely</td></tr>
<tr><td>

Probability adverbs:
perhaps, possibly, probably, presumably</td><td>

Frequency adverbs:
generally, usually, often, occasionally, seldom</td><td></td></tr>
</table>

The attributive verb you choose can also be a way of hedging. Consider the difference in the relative certainty of these two sentences:

A new report proves that some students may not be studying effectively for exams.

A new report hints that some students may not be studying effectively for exams.

This is all pretty exciting (if you ask me). Even with all of this though, especially in your longer essays, it can be easy to lose your voice among all the other voices (texts) you are using to answer the question, and we really don't want to lose you totally. One way to make sure you are always still included, is to give yourself the opening statement for each paragraph. That doesn't mean starting each paragraph with 'I think…', but instead you can make each opening sentence something you believe, or a stance you are taking, and then back this up with the evidence of other writers afterwards – using the attributive verbs to further connect their ideas with your opening statement. See chapter 6 for an idea of what this might look like.

There are some attributive verbs that get used a lot by students, but which don't really mean very much. Words like 'say' and 'mention' are almost as unhelpful as the word said. And the phrase 'according to' sounds quite academic, but really it just means said. Try using more specific attributive verbs to really help tell your story, to show how much you agree with an idea, and then get your opinion into your work.

Your lecturers are right, you shouldn't be using the word 'I' in academic writing and sentences like 'I think …' or 'In my opinion … ' are not academic in style and should be avoided. But unlike Elmore Leonard suggests, in academic writing it is really important to show you have a voice and to show both how you are contributing to the greater academic conversation, and how much you are agreeing with the ideas of other writers and researchers. Attributive verbs and hedging language are the best tools available to do this. So, stick your nose in, join the conversation and tell us what you think. Just don't write 'I think … '.

References

Centralia (n.d.). Verbs of attribution. Online Writing Lab (OWL) [Online] Available from: http://owl.centralia.edu/handouts/verbsatrib.pdf Accessed January 2019.

Leonard, E. (2010) Elmore Leonard's rules for writers. The Guardian [Online] Available from: https://www.theguardian.com/books/2010/feb/24/elmore-leonard-rules-for-writers Accessed March 2019.

CHAPTER 10

Writing: from the basics towards excellence

We've got down the basics now; how to outline different types of essays, how to synthesize texts to create complex critical writing and how to keep ourselves in our narrative by using attributive verbs and hedging. Our writing is starting to look pretty exciting, and your grades are going up. Is there any more we can do? Of course, there is, there is always more we can do. This chapter will look at some of the skills you need to continue advancing your writing towards excellence. We will look at some of the mechanics of writing such as grammar; better transitions; clarity and presenting your work. It might seem strange when talking about excellence in your writing to look back to grammar and syntax, these are in some ways the most basic parts of language and writing, but it's getting these right, and using them in a clever way, that will really make your work shine. Before we start on these though, let's remind ourselves of some general writing tips, because everything we have learned so far, and the stuff that is coming, can only work to its fullest if we have a few other more basic, or personal, things in place too.

Write where you are comfortable and write with your 'comfort food'

This might sound like an obvious piece of advice, but many students forget that thinking needs food, and more importantly it needs water. But also, your brain needs to be happy, and having the right foods and the right surroundings can make a real difference to your productivity – Don't spend so long getting these things right that it becomes procrastination, but listen to your body, give it the snacks it craves, and make sure you are well hydrated – you can always work off the excess chips after you graduate.

How to cite this book chapter:
Specht, D. 2019. *The Media And Communications Study Skills Student Guide.* Pp. 109–122. London: University of Westminster Press. DOI: https://doi.org/10.16997/book42.j. License: CC-BY-NC-ND 4.0

Before you worry about editing, just write!!

As we have already seen, everyone is a little different in the way in which they approach their writing, but as Edgar Allan Poe told us in chapter 4 the more we try and remember something, the quicker we are to forget it, so get outlines down fast, jot down ideas as they come, be they one word or whole paragraphs, and then come back later to make them perfect (you need to leave time for this of course). I have lost track of the number of ideas that have been lost to not remembering something that I wish I had written down.

Read grammar books

This chapter is going to give some general advice on some of the most common grammar issues you may face, but also taking some time to head back to grammar books, regardless of your English level, is a really quick and easy way to improve your writing. If you don't have a book yet, try Caplan's (2012) *Grammar Choices*, or Murphy and Smalzer's (2017) *Basic Grammar in Use*. Also, while you're reading academic texts you will find lots of unusual and complex grammar. Examine this, and try to emulate (not copy) it in your own writing. If it all seems too complex, then use grammar books to help you understand how this works and then you can use it in your own writings too, like a pro!

'Papers are never finished, but always due' as Kelly Gallagher, author of numerous books on writing, reminds us. This means that a cautious level of dropping perfectionism is required. You will be managing multiple essays and papers throughout your degree, and so it's important to balance these completing priorities. You need to be careful in managing your time, managing what is possible, and considering the relative weighting given to different papers. For example, missing a dissertation class because you are putting the final touches to a paper worth 10% of one module is probably a poor use of your time. So, plan carefully – Have you still not read chapter 2? Come on, go and do it now!

Work out what your average number of words written per day or hour is for assignments. This helps with time management.

STUDENT TIPS

Craig – MA Student

Practice makes perfect

A tired cliché? Maybe! But there is more than a slice of truth to this statement, and its important you realize that everyone is still practicing, we are all still shaping our writing, still developing our styles, still trying out new things. And you should be too. Try writing something every day, even if it doesn't make the final cut, that way you are constantly practicing and moving towards being perfect! It can though be hard to know if you are improving. Grades can give us some indication, but aren't always the best way for us to measure our own improvement. Instead we need to engage with critically reflecting on our own experiences using the skills we learned in chapter 6. Take some time out to look back over your work, what went well? Where were the issues? Have you made a conscious effort to work on those areas that you find more challenging? You could also get a friend to help with this – they need to be a good friend though, one who can be honest with you about your achievements, but not someone who is going to be nasty (they wouldn't be your friend anyway would they?). You could also speak with your personal tutor at the university, or another member of staff, about your progress – Of course their ideas might be more based on grades than your personal growth, so also take time to reflect on what they have said. Reflection is a really important part of practice makes perfect, so pop back to chapter 6 now and take some time out before coming back to grammar.

Okay. We have some general tips out of the way, let us get down to the nitty gritty of how to make your work shine through improving our grammar.

Grammar

As you know, this is not a grammar book, and I have already recommended that you go back to your grammar books to make sure you get these things right, but there are some specific issues that come up time and again in student writing, and they are the mistakes that make a difference between a basic piece of work and one that shows excellence – and we want excellence now. So, given that this chapter is called basics to excellence, it seems appropriate that I should share some grammar tips with you here. It might be tempting to skip this bit, none of us like grammar, but here is where your work can really shine. Even if you think you know English well, there are bound to be some things to help, so at the very least, practice your reading skills by not skipping this bit.

Note: Be careful, while I have tried to make these pages as useful as possible, they are a dangerously short guide to some very complex parts of English. The tips here will help with your essays, but for more detailed information, or if you are unsure, try a proper grammar book, something like Swan's (2005) *Practical English Usage.*

Caution

Prepositions: time and place

Prepositions, tiny little words that make a huge difference. In simple terms prepositions are used to show the relationship between other words, the problem is, they are hard to define on their own, and don't really mean very much at all out of context. The bigger problem is, your writing is all about showing relationships between words and ideas, so getting the prepositions right is a really important part of academic writing.

We mostly use prepositions along with other words, in what we call **prepositional phrase**s (starting to sound like a grammar book – keep with me here). There are millions of combinations of these words, but they normally follow the pattern of being a preposition followed by a *determiner* and an *adjective* or two, and then finished off nicely with a *noun* or *pronoun* (that is what we call the *object* of the sentence). When this is all put together it helps us to position objects, or ideas, in time and space, to give them a geographical or historical location. The easiest thing to do here is to look at some examples of the rules in action:

Prepositions of time: *at, on,* and *in*

We use *at* to designate specific times. *The train is due **at** 14:15 p.m*	We use *on* to designate days and dates. *My brother is coming **on** Monday.* *We're having a party **on** the 5ᵗʰ February.*	We use *in* for nonspecific times during a day, a month, a season, or a year. *He likes to jog **in** the morning.* *It's too hot **in** summer to run outside.* *She started the job **in** 1998.* *He's going to quit **in** September.*

Prepositions of place: *at, on,* and *in*

We use *at* for specific addresses. *Sarah lives **at** 67 New Street, London*	We use *on* to designate names of streets, avenues, etc. *Her house is **on** New Street*	And we use in for the names of land-areas (towns, counties, states, countries, and continents). *She lives **in** London.* *London is **in** England* *England is **in** the United Kingdom*

Prepositions of movement: *to* and *no preposition*

We use *to* in order to express movement toward a place. *They were walking **to** work together.* *She's going **to** the doctors this morning*	*Toward* and *towards* are also helpful prepositions to express movement. *We're moving **toward** the end of the class.* *This is a big step **towards** finishing your dissertation.*	With the words *home, downtown, uptown, inside, outside, downstairs, upstairs,* we use no preposition *My sister went upstairs* *He went home.* *They both went outside.*

Prepositions of time: *for* and *since*

We use *for* when we measure time (seconds, minutes, hours, days, months, years). *He held his breath **for** eight minutes.* *She's lived there **for** fifteen years.* *The internet has existed **for** three decades*	We use *since* with a specific date or time. *He's lived here **since** 1995.* *She's been waiting for her friend **since** six-thirty.*

Prepositions with nouns, adjectives, and verbs

Sometimes prepositions get really stuck to the words around them, like an annoying friend who doesn't know when to go home. In these cases, we have just given up, and let them basically become one word – If this was German, they would actually be one word, but this is English, so they are still two words, but they just have to be used together. This can happen with nouns, adjectives and with verbs, and like above, its easiest to show you how that happens – remember you don't need to learn this off the top of your head, use these pages while you are writing, and the rules will begin to stick:

NOUNS and PREPOSITIONS							
approve	of	fondness	for	need	for	concern	for
awareness	of	grasp	of	participation	in	confusion	about
belief	in	hatred	of	reason	for	desire	for
understanding	of	hope	for	respect	for		
		interest	in	success	in		

ADJECTIVES and PREPOSITIONS							
afraid	of	fond	of	proud	of	tired	of
angry	at	happy	about	similar	to	worried	about
aware	of	interested	in	sorry	for	made	of
capable	of	jealous	of	sure	of	married	to
careless	about	familiar	with				

VERBS and PREPOSITIONS							
apologize	for	give	up	prepare	for	work	for
ask	about	grow	up	study	for	worry	about
ask	for	look	for	talk	about	make	up
belong	to	look forward	to	think	about	pay	for
bring	up	look	up	trust	in	care	for
find	out						

Linkers and transitional words

All the ideas and writing methods we have discussed so far are great (if I do say so myself), but they are useless if you can't link ideas together well, leaving your writing looking overly simple. This is why it is essential to understand how *linking and transitional words* can be used to combine ideas in writing, as these words will make your writing flow and help you to express complex relationships between ideas. Many of these are small words, but just like our attributive verbs, they have many meanings and can change the whole tone of your writing very quickly – so it is important to take some time to check that you are using them correctly. Luckily for you I have included a whole load of them here for you. Remember to ensure you know what they *really* mean, by using a dictionary. Using different linking words can really change the way your essay reads, and can help you to show complex connections between ideas – you can quickly show agreement or disagreement between things you have read. Make sure you choose the right words though, because otherwise you will confuse the reader. Remember if you are unsure, use a dictionary to check the meaning of words before you use them.

Agreement/Addition/Similarity	The transition words like *also, in addition, and, likewise,* **add information**, **reinforce ideas**, and **express agreement** with preceding material.		
	in the first place not only ... but also as a matter of fact in like manner in addition coupled with in the same fashion/way first, second, third in the light of not to mention to say nothing of equally important by the same token	again to and also then equally identically uniquely like as too	moreover as well as together with of course likewise comparatively correspondingly similarly furthermore additionally
Opposition/Limitation/Contradiction	Transition phrases like *but, rather* and *or,* express that there is evidence to the **contrary** or point out **alternatives**, and thus introduce a change the line of reasoning (**contrast**).		
	although this may be true in contrast different from of course ..., but on the other hand on the contrary at the same time in spite of even so/though be that as it may then again above all in reality after all	but (and) still unlike or (and) yet while albeit besides as much as even though	although instead whereas despite conversely otherwise however rather nevertheless nonetheless regardless notwithstanding

Cause/Condition/Purpose	These transitional phrases present specific **conditions** or **intentions**.		
	in the event that granted (that) as/so long as on (the) condition (that) for the purpose of with this intention with this in mind in the hope that to the end that for fear that in order to seeing/being that in view of	If ... then unless when whenever while because of as since while lest	in case provided that given that only/even if so that so as to owing to inasmuch as due to

Examples/Support/Emphasis	These transitional devices (like *especially*) are used to introduce examples as **support**, to indicate **importance** or as an **illustration** so that an idea is cued to the reader.		
	in other words to put it differently for one thing as an illustration in this case for this reason to put it another way that is to say with attention to by all means important to realize another key point first thing to remember most compelling evidence must be remembered point often overlooked to point out on the positive side on the negative side with this in mind	notably including like to be sure namely chiefly truly indeed certainly surely markedly such as especially explicitly specifically expressly surprisingly frequently significantly particularly	in fact in general in particular in detail for example for instance to demonstrate to emphasize to repeat to clarify to explain to enumerate

Effect/Consequence/Result	Some of these transition words (*thus, then, accordingly, consequently, therefore, henceforth*) are time words that are used to show that *after* a particular time there was a **consequence** or an **effect**. Note that *for* and *because* are placed before the cause/reason. The other devices are placed before the consequences or effects.		
	as a result under those circumstances in that case for this reason in effect	for thus because the then hence	consequently therefore thereupon forthwith accordingly henceforth
Conclusion/Summary / Restatement	These transition words and phrases **conclude**, **summarize** and/or **restate** ideas, or indicate a final **general statement**. Also, some words (like *therefore*) from the **effect/consequence** category can be used to summarize.		
	as can be seen generally speaking in the final analysis all things considered as shown above in the long run given these points as has been noted in a word for the most part	after all in fact in summary in conclusion in short in brief in essence to summarize on balance altogether overall ordinarily usually	by and large to sum up on the whole in any event in either case all in all obviously ultimately definitely

Adapted from Smart-Words (2013)

Articles

Another place where students often experience problems is with their articles. These can be much harder in English than in other languages. Even English-speaking people can rarely explain to you how they work, go on, go and ask one. Go on, don't be shy. See, they had no idea what you were talking about did they? There are three articles in English are **a**, **an** and **the**, and you need to decide noun-by-noun which one of the articles to use. In fact, there are four choices to make, because sometimes no article is necessary. The issue is that native speakers and writers use the articles correctly without thinking, and so mistakes really jump out, even if they can't explain why. So, here is a quick guide to using articles like a native speaker.

The first step in choosing the right article is knowing if the noun is **countable** or **uncountable** *in its context*. If the noun **can** have a number in front of it (*1 teacher, 3 books, 76 computers, 1,000,000 people*) it is countable. And so conversely an *uncountable* noun is a noun that **cannot** have a number put in front of it (1 water, 2 lucks, 10 airs, 21 oils, 39 informations all sound wrong). Once you have worked out this, you can simply follow these rules very helpfully laid out in the blog *englishedubloginsal* (n.d.):

Uncountable nouns

- You cannot say **a/an** with an uncountable noun.
- You cannot put a number in front of an uncountable noun. (You cannot make an uncountable noun plural.)
- You use an uncountable noun with no article if you mean that thing *in general.*
- You use **the** with an uncountable noun when you are talking about a particular example of that thing.

Countable nouns

- You can put a number in front of a count noun. (You can make a count noun plural.)
- You can put both **a/an** and **the** in front of a count noun.
- You **must** put an article in front of a singular count noun.
- You use a plural count noun with no article if you mean all or any of that thing.
- You usually use **a/an** with a count noun the first time you say or write that noun.
- You use **the** with count nouns:
    - the second and subsequent times you use the noun in a piece of speech or writing
    - when the listener knows what you are referring to (maybe because there is only one of that thing)
- You use **an** (not **a**) when the next word (adverb, adjective, noun) starts with a vowel sound.

Caution	• The rules cited above apply both when there is (or there is not) an adjective before the noun.
	• Some nouns can be either *countable* or *uncountable*; which depends on the meaning and context:
	○ Do you have paper? I want to draw a picture. (uncountable = a sheet of paper)
	○ Can you get me **a** paper when you're at the shop? (countable = a newspaper)
	• Uncountable nouns are often preceded by phrases such as: *a load of ... (luck), a piece of ... (chocolate), a bottle of ... (orange juice), a grain of ... (wheat).*

Tenses

Another area of English that we often get wrong is the tenses, and this is a particular problem in academic writing. Most of what we write is in a past tense (apart from proposals about forthcoming work), but we need to change tense depending on whether a debate or idea is ongoing or if the authors are alive or not. Here is a quick reference guide to help you with the tenses. Remember though, this is just a quick guide, and you might need to check a grammar book too.

Tense	Example	Explanation
Simple Present	I use Twitter every day.	Here you want to say that it happens regularly.
Present Progressive	I'm using Twitter now.	Here you want to say that it is happening at the moment.
Simple Past	I used Twitter yesterday.	You did it yesterday, it happened in the past.
Past Progressive	I was using Twitter the whole evening.	You were doing it in the past. It's not sure whether the action was finished or not.
Present Perfect	I have just used Twitter.	You have just finished it. So, it has a connection to the present. Maybe your laptop is still on.
Present Perfect Progressive	I have been using Twitter for 2 hours.	You want to say how long you have been doing it. You started in the past and it continues up to the present.

Tense	Example	Explanation
Past Perfect	I had used Twitter before Susan came.	The two actions are related to each other: you had finished with Twitter, and after that Susan arrived.
Past Perfect Progressive	I had been using Twitter when Susan came.	Here you want to point out how long you had been doing it before Susan came.
Will-future	I will use Twitter next week.	This is a prediction; you can probably do something else.
Going to-future	I'm going to use Twitter this afternoon.	This is a plan you've made.
Future Progressive	I will be using Twitter next Sunday.	You do it every Sunday (as usual).
Future Perfect	I will have used Twitter by tomorrow.	You will have done it before tomorrow.
Conditional Simple	I would use Twitter.	You'll probably do it.
Conditional Progressive	I would be using Twitter.	You'll probably do it. Here you concentrate more on the progress of the action.
Conditional Perfect	I would have used Twitter.	You'll probably have finished using Twitter at a special time in the future. Here you concentrate on the fact (Twitter).
Conditional Perfect Progressive	I would have been using Twitter.	You'll probably have finished using Twitter at a special time in the future. Here you concentrate on the progress of using (Twitter).

Adapted from English-Hilfen (n.d.)

Nominalization

We can also turn our writing into something more professional sounding by using nominalization, which is easier to do than it is to say. A key part of academic writing is the process of nominalization turns verbs (actions) into nouns (things, concepts, or people). This makes the tone of your writing sounds more abstract and more formal. So basically nominalization, like the use of passive voice, gives the impression of being a proper academic.

How to do normalization

Nominalization allows you to discuss more abstract concepts by taking the focus off the action and making the action into a concept or idea. To do this;

1. Identify the event/action
2. Change this verb to a noun form
3. Make this noun form definite (if appropriate)
   — This is now the head noun.
4. Add 'of what' to the head noun (if necessary).

✗ Online hate crime <u>was increasing</u> rapidly and the police <u>were becoming concerned</u>.

Becomes…

✓ The rapid **increase** in online hate crime was causing **concern** amongst the police.

✗ The Guardian <u>leaked</u> the Panama Papers in 2016. This was the immediate <u>cause</u> of a new wave of investigative journalism

Becomes…

✓ The Guardian's **leaking** of the Panama Papers in 2016 **caused** a new wave of investigative journalism.

Unity

And finally, we have to ensure that everything has unity. Unity is related to two main aspects; every sentence is related to the main topic, and every paragraph has cohesion. This can be done through the use of pronouns, repetition of key nouns, synonyms, antonyms, and transition signals. Here are a set of examples of how to use each of these:

Pronouns: Johannes Gutenberg invented the first practical printing press in 1436, and continued to refine <u>**it**</u> until 1440. <u>**This**</u> resulted in the rapid production and dissemination of affordable books, which fostered unprecedented development of the sciences, arts and religion.

Repetition: Johannes Gutenberg invented the first practical printing press in 1436, and continued to refine it until 1440. The new <u>**printing press**</u> resulted in the rapid production and dissemination of affordable books, which fostered unprecedented development of the sciences, arts and religion.

Synonyms: Johannes Gutenberg invented the first practical printing press in 1436, and continued to refine it until 1440. This **mechanical innovation** resulted in the rapid production and dissemination of affordable books, which fostered unprecedented development of the sciences, arts and religion.

Antonyms: Johannes Gutenberg invented the first practical printing press in 1436, and continued to refine it until 1440. Without the rapidly increased production and dissemination of affordable books, that ensued, development of the sciences, arts and religion would have **languished**.

Transitional signals: Johannes Gutenberg invented the first practical printing press in 1436, and continued to refine it until 1440. **Consequently**, the rapid production and dissemination of affordable books, which fostered unprecedented development of the sciences, arts and religion, was possible.

*   *   *

We are heading towards the end of this book, and we have many of the mechanics of writing sorted, from reading, referencing, grammar and unity. We now need to know how we actually apply all these things in the framework of an essay, or a larger dissertation piece of work. Over the next chapters, we will start to bring together the different elements of writing, and introduce some final ideas.

References

Caplan, N. A. (2012). *Grammar choices for graduate and professional writers.* Ann Arbor, University of Michigan Press.

englishedubloginsal (n.d.). Articles a, an, the. English Edublog –INSAL – Ahuachapán. Available at http://englishedubloginsal.blogspot.com

English-Hilfen (n.d.). Sentences change their meanings [online]. Available from: https://www.englisch-hilfen.de/en/grammar/tenses_satz.htm

Murphy, R. & Smalzer, W. R. (2017). *Basic grammar in use: Self-study reference and practice for students of English. Student's book.* Stuttgart, Ernst Klett Sprachen.

Smart-Words (2013) Transition Words [Online] Available from: https://www.smart-words.org/linking-words/transition-words.html Accessed January 2019.

Swan, M. (2005). *Practical english usage.* Oxford, Oxford University Press.

CHAPTER 11

Writing questions for research projects

At some point in your studies you will be asked to write your own research questions. Something like; *Why did the chicken cross the road?* This is a classic, and clearly a very funny joke. However, it would not make for a very good research question. We might want to know why the chicken crossed the road, but this question is too broad and does not define the segments of the analysis: the question does not address which chicken or which road, and thus isn't a useful question at all for research. When you come to write your dissertation, and in some cases for other assignments too, you will have to write your own research question. This is no easy task. You will hear what sounds like a million contradictions as you try to write your research questions; they are too broad, or too narrow, not original, too original. So how do we get them, right? Well let's start with this strange idea:

DAVID FOSTER WALLACE

David Foster Wallace, an American writer, is quite right, a fish doesn't know it is in water. What does he mean by this? And how would this help us in

How to cite this book chapter:
Specht, D. 2019. *The Media And Communications Study Skills Student Guide.* Pp. 123–131. London: University of Westminster Press. DOI: https://doi.org/10.16997/book42.k. License: CC-BY-NC-ND 4.0

answering and writing questions? If you met a fish and asked them to explain what water is, they would reply, 'what is what?'. They are so surrounded by it that it is impossible for them to see it. They can't see it until they get outside of it, to look back at it from the outside – not easy for a fish to do. The same is true in examining society, media and communications. We are so surrounded by them that it is hard to step out and look back in – but this is just what we need to do when we are answering questions, and even more so when we are writing our own questions. To fully understand questions about society we can't look from our own experience or personal knowledge, but must look from the experience of all society and by drawing upon the knowledge of all scholars in the field so as to add to that knowledge – we need to be like a fish who can see the water… or something like that.

Let's take this idea and apply it to our chicken joke example to see how we might develop a research question.

We could improve the chicken question by making it more specific, and ask something like;

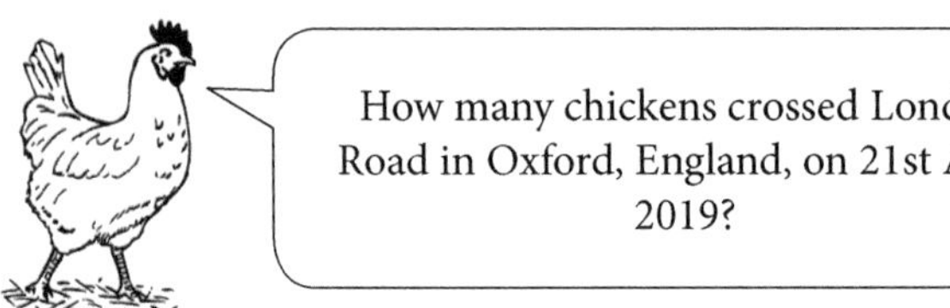

This is better, but this doesn't really work as a research question either, as you could maybe answer this just by doing an internet search. And you could answer this question in one sentence, or even one word. It does not leave room for analysis, an important part of your work. It could, however, become data for a larger argument, but that doesn't make it a suitable research question alone.

Let's have another go:

Now we are getting somewhere, this is a much more precise question. This question means you can take a stand about which factors are significant, and allows you to argue to what degree the results are significant or not, and how much influence they have on chickens.

Those examples are all well and good, but how do we actually formulate a good question and research idea? To do that we need to understand your position within the research environment. By the time you come to write your own research questions you will have completed much of your studies and are already a researcher, and you should be starting to act like one too… even if that is a little scary at the beginning. Because you are a researcher it means your research question will be sitting within the broader research environment. You are now a cog in the wider world of research.

You have a whole load of ideas about how the world works, but now you are part of the wider research environment, you need to create **rigorous** research – that is research that is extremely thorough and careful – and you need to understand the research carried out by others. You also need to have an outcome that is related to practice, be this business, society, a company or a theoretical understanding of a phenomena. Between these sits your research, which through a rigorous design approach and being practice based, also becomes **relevant**.

The key here is that by making our research relevant and rigorous it goes beyond being something that you personally are interested in, and becomes something that the wider research community, business sector or society, is interested in knowing. And that is not only the key to writing a good research question, it is also key to writing an excellent dissertation.

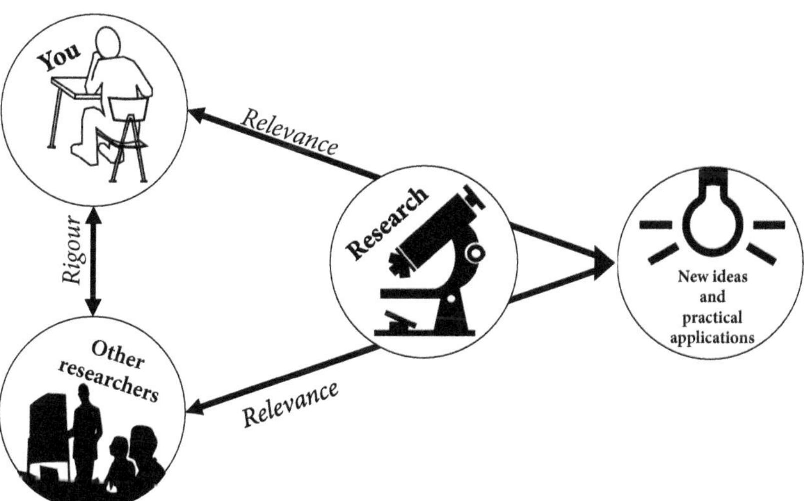

Generating ideas

It is usually simple to identify a theme or a general area of interest. However, the process of arriving at an idea that goes beyond your own questioning of the world, and developing the final form of a research question is more difficult and requires you to narrow the area of general interest, making it more specific. First, let's look at how to have an idea for a theme, and then we will narrow it down.

Start by thinking about your interests and motivation. This could be related to your future career, the most interesting book or article you've read, or perhaps a media company, type of content, technology or platform you love. You may also want to consider your own knowledge – perhaps about a company you are with or have worked at, a job you have done or a business, or a place you know well. Go back to look at what inspired you to join the Masters programme.

Another way to think of a research topic is to think about your **question as a problem**. This means considering a problem where the solution is something that is debatable and to which there might be a number of different solutions, but which is also something that the wider research community (not just you) might want to know about.

So, a bad question might be improved like this;

Bad	Has the internet affected sales of daily newspapers?	Here there is no debate to be had, much like our chicken example a simple internet search could give us the answer.
Good	How can news organizations respond to the threats posed by new media?	Here there is a lot of debate, and there is a lot of discussion to be had. Furthermore, it is a really important issue that lots of people would like to know the answer to and which would help contribute to the wider research environment.

A really good way to see if your research question is suitable in relation to the wider research environment is to apply …

The 'so what?' test

To do this test, have a think about what interests or inspires your about media and communications and then try completing these three sentences in order to see if your research question holds up to the standards mentioned above;

TASK

Try it yourself:

Topic: I am studying ____

Question: Because I want to answer _______________________________

____?

Significance: In order to help solve real world problem:

If you can't complete all three sections of this then you need to go back to the drawing board with your question. And if your friends or lecturers ask 'so what? Who cares?' about any of these three, then I'm afraid that, too means going back to the drawing board, because your topic just isn't of interest to the wider research environment or the world at large… a pain I know, however your research needs to be interesting to more than just you.

TOP TIPS

Try free writing

Free writing is a prewriting technique in which you write continuously for a set period of time without thinking about spelling, grammar or topic. It is really good for getting ideas going and to draw out thoughts from deeper in your mind. To do free writing:

➢ Get a pen and paper.
➢ Set a timer for 2 minutes (you can set it for longer, but start with two minutes).
➢ When the timer starts write everything that comes into your mind. Don't stop writing until the alarm sounds, don't censor yourself, don't worry about spelling and don't stop to make corrections.
➢ Once the time is up, take a breather.
➢ Now look back at what you have written and pull out any useful ideas.

Now we have a topic we need to really focus that topic 'in'. We often use the image of the funnel to help represent the intellectual process of moving from a theme to a more focused subject.

Look at the example below which demonstrates this narrowing process:

Selecting a theme
(Facebook (XXL))

Narrowing the focus
(Using Facebook to plan meetings (XL))

Becoming more specific
(Using Facebook to plan meeting between new mothers (L))

Defining a well focused topic
(Using Facebook to plan offline meetings between new single mothers in South London (OK))

Now it is time for you to try and write a research question of your own, think about:

- ✓ What will be studied
- ✓ Who will be studied
- ✓ When will they be studied
- ✓ Where will they be studied
- ✓ How it will be studied
- ✓ Why it will be studied.

And then borrow this template to shape the question:
(How/Why/What)(Who?) (Where?) (What?) (Why?)? (How?)(When?).

EXAMPLE How do new single mothers living in South London use Facebook to create offline community groups, and what impact does this have on childcare? A qualitative study of 75 new mothers through the summer of 2018.

TASK **Try it yourself:**

How/Why/What_________________ Who?_________________

Where?_____________ What?_____________ Why?_____________?

How?_______________ When?_______________.

Research question checklist

- ❑ My research question is something that I, and other people, will care about.
- ❑ I am able to take a stance in relation to the predicted outcome.
- ❑ My research tries to solve a problem, or puts a new spin on old ideas.
- ❑ My research question isn't too broad or too narrow.
- ❑ I have enough time to undertake this research deeply and properly.
- ❑ I have enough resources to carry out this work (money, time, people).
- ❑ I am able to measure the outcomes of my research.
- ❑ I am aware of contradicting arguments around my research question.

- ✕ Research questions that are not asked.
- ✕ Research questions that are not answerable.
- ✕ Research questions that have Yes/No answers.
- ✕ Research questions whose answers don't produce any new knowledge.
- ✕ Research questions that don't have 'symmetry of outcome'.
- ✕ Research questions that are too broad.
- ✕ Research questions that are too narrow.
- ✕ Research questions that include presumptions.

REMEMBER:

While a good research question allows the writer to take an arguable position, it DOES NOT leave room for ambiguity.

The wrong research question leads to wasted time and effort!

Problem: You're working hard, but you don't seem to be making progress. You're spending lots of time on side issues, changing your mind, finding lots of tangents that look interesting.

Solution: This may be a sign that your question is not clear enough. Try to get it down to a few short sentences. What are you trying to find? Keep asking the 'so what?' question. It might be useful to explain what your research is about to someone. They don't have to be an expert.

Problem: As you get immersed in the literature and research, lots of interesting topics emerge. You spend a lot of time on tangential issues here are endless interesting questions to answer, but you only have time to do one.

Solution: Once your question is clear, write it out in big letters on one sheet of paper and stick it prominently near your computer. As you get distracted, read the question, and decide if what you are reading or working on is directly relevant to your question.

Doing a Masters degree is all about questions, it is about reading the answers to other people's questions in texts; about asking questions in class; about answering questions in essays; about writing questions for dissertations. So many questions! So, understanding how questions work is really important for getting along in your studies. When your professors set you questions to answer, they have a very particular idea in their mind about how these essays should look, and you can get inside their minds (don't stay too long) by understanding the language they use when they pose these questions. As you come to write your own questions, ensure you follow the formulas in this book, and look at examples from published works. And of course, if you are unsure about something … Ask a question! Not asking a question might actually be more foolish, as Alice Walker American novelist and social activist reminds us;

ALICE WALKER

Reference

Jenkins, H. (2006) Eight Traits of the New Media Landscape. Henry Jenkins [Online] Available from: http://henryjenkins.org/blog/2006/11/eight_traits_of_the_new_media.html Accessed January 2019.

CHAPTER 12

Empirical research skills

At the end of the last chapter we reached the final part of the book. But what's this? Two more chapters? How and why? I thought we were done! Well in many ways we are. But there still looms one large project for you to undertake in your degree, that is the dissertation or thesis. That task is designed to bring together all the skills we have looked at so far, as well as all your knowledge and ideas from the course, putting them together in one big piece of original writing, fully designed by you. In the very final chapter of the book (13) we will look at how to bring these things together, but first there is just one last skill that we need before we can undertake a dissertation or thesis, and that is knowing how to carry out empirical research.

There are loads of full length books on this subject, so this chapter will only offer a quick overview of the skills you need for doing research. We will go through the process of designing your research and then look at a couple of the methods most commonly used, including key techniques, interviews, surveys, content analysis, digital ethnography, and some basic network analysis. You should though consider this a springboard to using other texts to help you perfect this.

How to cite this book chapter:
Specht, D. 2019. *The Media And Communications Study Skills Student Guide*. Pp. 133–151. London: University of Westminster Press. DOI: https://doi.org/10.16997/book42.l. License: CC-BY-NC-ND 4.0

Let's start, where we should always start, in designing a research project, and that is with a couple of rather complex sounding words, these are **Epistemology** and **Ontology**. Don't panic – you already know what these are (kind of). In a very simple way, epistemology refers to questions about what knowledge is and how it can be acquired. Ontology is the philosophical study of the nature of being, becoming, existence, or reality, as well as the basic categories of being and their relations. Okay, that still sounds a bit complex. But, they are both things we already consider, although we probably don't think about them much until our professors ask us to. Let's try one more simplification, *Ontology* is about how you think the world works, and *Epistemology* is how you think we can study it (Phew! Got it!). This will affect our methodology.

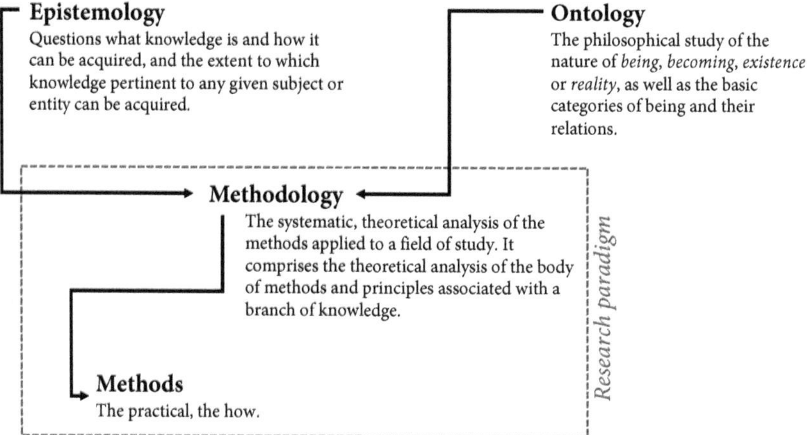

Figure 12.1: Methodologies.

Before we look at that though, let's try and explain this a little further. Brechin and Siddell (2000) highlight three different ways of knowing about our world: There is **empirical knowing**, the kind which is based on quantitative or qualitative research study – like in your thesis. There is **theoretical knowing**, which uses different theoretical frameworks for thinking about a problem, sometimes informed by research, this is basically your literature review. And there is **experiential knowing** (also known as 'tacit') that is knowledge built up over a number of years of practice and experience. This is the one we experience as children when we learn not to put our hands on the hot oven more than once. We also continue to learn this way all through our lives. It is not easy to keep these separate though, and there is a lot of interaction between them, but this chapter is mostly dealing with that first type, the empirical knowing. It is your literature review that deals mostly with theoretical knowing, and your reflections on the success of your project that employs more experiential knowing.

PAULO FREIRE

Methods and methodologies… what's the difference?

In class you will hear your tutors talking about methods and methodologies. This can become rather confusing; the words sound similar and in many ways they have similar meanings. Worse, as this passage from the *American Heritage Dictionary* (1992 edition) states:

> *in recent years … 'methodology' has been increasingly used as a pretentious substitute for 'method' in scientific and technical contexts. This usage may have been fostered in part by the tendency to use the adjective 'methodological' to mean 'pertaining to methods,' inasmuch as the regularly formed adjective 'methodical' has been preempted to mean 'orderly, systematic.' But the misuse of methodology obscures an important conceptual distinction between the tools of scientific investigation (properly 'methods') and the principles that determine how such tools are deployed and interpreted—a distinction that the scientific and scholarly communities, if not the wider public, should be expected to maintain.*

Well now, that makes things much worse doesn't it. People mix-up the words all the time. It is though unlikely your professor will, but in other contexts these mix-ups can lead to confusion, so let's make things simple:

Methodology	Method
Explains why you are going to undertake research in a particular way. It draws upon literature, epistemologies and links your methods to the theories and literature review.	How you will do the research. E.g. interview, survey.

As you can see, without a methodology you won't be able to tell the reader why you are using a particular method, and that is the bit that gives you the most marks. When it comes to writing a dissertation, the markers are rarely overly interested in **what** you do, but are much more interested in **why** you do it. One of the main justifications you will need to make is about whether you are using quantitative, qualitative or mixed methods approaches – but what are those? Well, read on to find out.

The methodology: quantitative or qualitative research?

Debates have been going on for ever about which is better, quantitative or qualitative, but what do they actually mean? Well in very simple terms, quantitative research normally deals with numbers, and qualitative works more with things that can't be counted so easily. The debates about which is better rage on because each has its own strengths and weaknesses, and worse, these change depending on what we are doing, upon our *epistemological* approach and our *ontological* outlook. You may not feel like this history is all that important, but is very interesting. Sadly, though we don't have time to look at it in this book, so you are saved from a history lesson, instead we will answer the question you actually want to know the answer to – which method should you use?

Figure 12.2: Quantitative or qualitative research?

Quantitative research

Quantitative research is the numbers one. It is often seen as more scientific, and it is used much more in the hard (or true) sciences or in experiments (the kind where you have to wear a white coat). It uses very traditional mathematical techniques and statistics (eek) to make very strong, and often conclusive, sets of results. While it is often used in those fields, it is also very useful for us in media and communications, and the social sciences more broadly. The methods use very standard formats, which means we can repeat them quite easily to show comparisons or to check results match in other places. We could use quantitative research to analyze social media data, to look at the content of films, to unlock the secrets of media management or to conduct audience surveys, as well as many other things. You will need a basic understanding of maths, but don't go running for the hills just yet, let's see the advantages and drawbacks of quantitative research:

Quantitative methods	
Advantages	**Disadvantages**
Quantitative research is very good at helping us to reach a definitive answer, at least about the sample group we are working with. It can be used to prove or disprove a hypothesis, and to show mathematically the degree to which this is true. Quantitative methods have also not changed for a very long time, and so they are easy to reproduce, and when you write about them people will understand what you are writing about. And if you do it correctly it means that people can replicate your work, which is often seen as making the work more rigorous and 'proper'.	Quantitative methods can be difficult, expensive and time consuming. While doing a survey or counting content might seem like easy options, at degree level you need to collect very large amounts of data, and from the correct sample (more on that later). This isn't always very easy, and getting enough data to make a statistically supported statement can take a lot of work. Talking of statistics, you will also need a pretty decent grasp of Maths to be able to analyze your data. The final disadvantage is that often we are looking at social phenomena, and these issues are more complex that the yes/no answers that quantitative methods produce.

Qualitative research

Qualitative research is even older than quantitative. The ancient Greek philosophers would pass the time observing the world around them, trying to make sense of what was happening, and why. These methods are often used to study human behaviour, feelings, habits or emotions. It relies much more on talking with people, or observing how they interact, be this in real life or online, and include things like interviews and focus groups. We normally use qualitative methods when we aren't sure what we are going to find out, to explore new ideas that might then lead us to develop a hypothesis for quantitative research later. Qualitative methods are great, but because they are so flexible, they can be hard to design well, and often can't be repeated. Let's have a closer look at the advantages and disadvantages of qualitative methods:

Qualitative methods	
Advantages	**Disadvantages**
Qualitative methods are really well suited to projects where you won't get a yes or no answer, or things were the results are going to be more complex or individual. In many ways qualitative methods are easier, and because of how they are designed they almost always bring in data – even no data is interesting to qualitative researchers because they can ask, why didn't that happen? Samples sizes don't have to be so big, although they still need to be carefully designed, and this can make qualitative methods cheaper and quicker too.	Despite what that column to the left says, there are a great many difficulties in designing and carrying out qualitative methods. They require a lot of planning and careful thought to be able to get them right and to ensure your results mean something. They will also only give you a general feeling about something, you can't produce a definitive answer, and this can also mean your personal opinion can affect the results. Finally, the answer you do produce will normally be limited only to the small group you have worked with, rather than being able to say it is true for the whole population.

Mixed methods

You might have also heard about a mixed methods approach, this is simply the combining of qualitative and quantitative methods in a way in which they support each other and help you to reach a more concrete conclusion. They can be combined in a whole range or ways, but it is most common to undertake qualitative research first (perhaps an interview), to find out new information, and then to follow up with quantitative (perhaps a survey) to see if these findings apply to a larger population. The great guru of mixed methods is perhaps John Creswell (2013), and you might want to take a look at one of his books on the subject. Of course, your lecturers might have another book they prefer you to use, so be sure to check your reading lists.

Creswell (2013) also offers us some great advice about how to write our methodology chapters. You can use the template below to help you. Thank you, John!

> **EXAMPLE** Creswell has given us a really helpful guide about how to write your methodology:
>
> **Creswell's (2013) script for quantitative studies**
>
> The theory I will use is __________(*theory name*). It was developed by __________ (*origin, source, developer of the theory*), and it was used to study __________ (*topic where one finds the theory applies*). The theory indicated that ___________ (*identify propositions of hypotheses*). As applied to my study, this theory hold that I would expect my independent variable(s) ____________ to influence or explain my dependent variables ______________ because ____________ (*provide rationale based on the logic of the theory*).
>
> **Creswell's (2013) script adapted for qualitative studies**
>
> The purpose of this ____________ (*phenomenological, grounded theory, ethnographic, historical, case*) study is to ____________ (*Understand? Describe? Develop? Discover?*) the ____________ (*central phenomenon of the study*) for ____________ (*the participants*) at ____________ (*the site*). At this stage in the research, ____________ (*central phenomenon*) will be generally defined as ____________ (*a general definition of the central concept*). The theory guiding this study is ______________ (*identify theory and cite theorist*) as it ____________ (*explain the relationship between the theory and your focus of inquiry*).

Methods

Now we have decided which methodological approach you are going to take, let's have a quick look at some common methods. Remember, this is just a very quick overview of the methods. There are loads we could use for example:

As this isn't a methods book though, we will only be able to look very quickly at a few quick tips for designing different types of research. You should keep in mind that these are almost dangerously short introductions to these methods and that you should also consult some other more methods-based books to help you get these right. However, over the next few pages we present some simple flow diagrams of the processes of carrying out some of the more common types of research methods in the field of media and communications. We will cover the more familiar interviews and surveys, both of which are a lot harder to do right than any of us think – sorry to bring bad news. We will also have a look at a couple of less familiar examples including content analysis, which examines the way in which different texts are formed, designed and understood, and what this might mean about how they represent the world and how the world works. Following that we will look at some very basic network analysis and the tools you might use to undertake this.

Digital methodologies

The methods discussed over the next few pages might also be used as part of a **Digital Ethnography** methodology. This way of working, which is also sometimes called netnography or virtual ethnography or even cyber ethnography, is at its simplest a way of conducting research about the lived experience in the online world. It borrows research methods from ethnography and adapts them to help with the study of communities and cultures created through computer-mediated social interaction. Tools of analysis such as Network Analysis and Content Analysis can form an important part of a Digital Ethnographic research project. For more information on this kind of work see Pink (2016) or Murthy (2008; 2011; 2013).

Each of the methods is covered in several pages, which is nowhere near long enough to discuss all of the issues and benefits of each, but is just the right size to help you choose which methods you might like to explore further, and is also the right size to photocopy and stick on your wall near your desk, or to slip in your pocket if you need a quick guide to that information while you are out and about doing your research. Right, let's get started … first up, interviews:

Interviews

Interviews are a qualitative method and are used to collect data and ideas that cannot be easily described using numbers. They seek to explore feelings and emotions or to explain why something has happened.

Sampling for interviews involves deciding how many people, and which people you will interview. You need to speak to enough people from the population for your work to be valid. If your topic is very narrow, but deep, you may not need many interviewees at all, instead you can focus on those with direct experience. For broader projects you may need more people. The key is to ensure you have spoken with the right number of people to be able to provide an answer to your research question.

There are three main **types of interview**.
- Semi-structured interviews are most common. The researcher has a list of questions for the respondent, and asked similar questions to everyone, but also allows them to tell their own versions of events (without too many tangents).
- Structured interviews follow a very strict pattern of questions, often with much shorter answers.
- Unstructured interviews actually take a lot of planning, but they allow the respondent to lead the conversation more.

Preparing to conduct interviews takes time. You need to ensure you are clear about the aims of the interviews, and also make sure this is explained to any interviewees so they are fully aware – and you will need their consent if they agree to the interview.
You should also prepare an interview guide. Design your questions so they help answer your research question. Think about the order of the questions – use easier questions to help get the conversation flowing, don't start with very personal or sensitive questions. You should also check your questions are easy to understand and don't require too much additional explanation. You should practice on some friends, and don't be afraid to change the questions slightly after your first interview if things don't go to plan. Finally, it is important to design your questions so questions aren't leading – these are questions where you accidently persuade people to give a type of answer.

As part of our preparation we can consider different **types of questions**. Kvale (1996) describes nine types of questions, and that text is a good one to read if you are doing interviews. Let's look at some of these;

- Introducing questions, just to get things stated
- Probing questions try and get more detail from people
- Follow-up questions encourage the interviewee to say more on a topic
- Direct questions, are quick, with simple yes or no kind of answers
- Indirect questions seek to get true opinions on the topic
- Specifying questions ask for more specifics on what happened following a story from the interviewee
- Structuring questions help to move the conversation forwards; interpreting questions will help you to clarify points
- Silence, often forgotten, but allows the respondent time to think and answer and for you to really listen to them

It is important to keep a **record of the interview**. Ideally you will record the interview with a digital recorder, but you can only do this with the consent of the interviewee. If they don't want to be recorded then ask if you can take notes. And remember if something is 'off record' or they don't want you to use their name then you will need to respect that, regardless of how juicy the information is.

Following the interview you may need to **transcribe** what has been said. How much of this you do will depend on your university and on how you will analyze the interview. Warning: Transcription is a very time consuming process.

You also need to consider your analysis. Will you simply pick out key quotes to illustrate your ideas or will you turn your interview into quantitative data by labelling key words and phrases allowing you to count instances of ideas across multiple interviews? This is what is called coding an interview and there are lots of guides as to how to do this, software like Nvivo also really helps. It is worth considering how you will analyze your data before you start any interviews. Remembering that just like other parts of the method, the analysis should be designed as to best answer your research question, not just what seems fun.

Surveys

Surveys are a quantitative method and are generally used to collect data that is more rigid, and which and be easily turned into numbers. They require at least some basic maths skills to be able to analyze well.

Choosing who you will survey, **sampling**, is really important. You should only give your survey to people who will help answer your research question, and every respondent should be hand chosen (either through random or purposive sampling). You can't just give a survey to anyone, and see if they fit the demographics later, you need to plan things a little more than that – especially if you are doing your survey online, where you should add 'qualifying' questions.

When **designing your survey**, you need to think carefully about the types of questions you are asking. Make sure you start with easier questions, with short answers, and leave open-ended questions with longer answers, and personal information until the very end. Other types of questions you might like to use are:

Multiple choice: Here you give a range of possible answers. You must make sure you include all possibilities here.

Ordinal scale questions: Here you ask people to rank ideas or a range of items. For example, 'Place the following in order of importance when choosing a social media platform … '

Interval scale questions: This is a very common type of question and asks people on a scale how they feel about something. 'On a scale of 1 – 10, how satisfied are you with this book, 10 being very satisfied, and 1 being very unsatisfied' You must make your scale balanced.

Ratio scale question: This asks people to give you an measurable answer; often this is used with ordinal scales too. (e.g. How many hours are you on Instagram each day?).

Open question: here you ask the respondent to give you much more information. People are often less keen to answer these as they take longer. E.g. 'Why is this your favourite class, explain?'

When you are **conducting the survey**, it is important you do this in a well-planned way. You must make sure you introduce yourself and the research and ensure that the respondents know what will happen with their data. Respondents should have the option to skip questions or to end the survey and withdraw their information. You should also always test your survey on a small group before sending it out. This will help you find any small (or big) mistakes).

When you finish collecting the data, you need to **analyze** the information. While some simple graphs can help, at a Masters level you should be considering applying some statistical analysis to your data. While it is beyond the scope of this book to teach you statistics, the chart below will help you in choosing which statistical tools to use on your data. Also consider using software such as SPSS, which is a little more powerful that other spreadsheet tools.

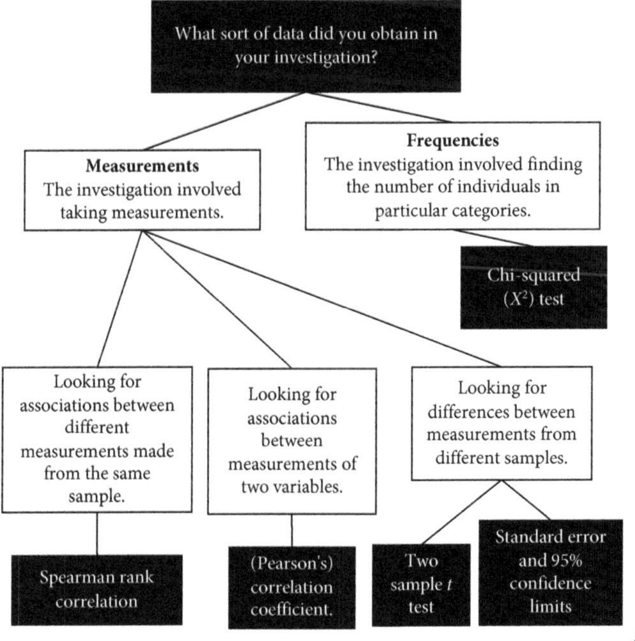

Content analysis

Content analysis is a way of examining the presence of words or images within a text (in its broad definition), and for us to be able to examine the relationships between these words.

Content analysis has many **uses**. It can be used to examine a huge range of things, including; books; book chapters, essays, interviews, films, Twitter, newspapers, articles, historical documents, speeches, conversations, advertising, theatre, paintings or other visuals. Almost anything where there is some form of communication involved. It can detect propaganda, identify intentions of writers, and can see differences in types of communication, and there's loads more besides those things…

As with any of the methods here, the **sample** you choose to analyze is very important. You need to think about how many texts you will analyze, and over what time periods. It would be impossible to examine every newspaper for the last year, or every YouTube video or Tweet. So how do you decide what to include? What about just Sundays, or just front pages? If you are doing analysis on interviews, are they yours or are they someone else's? Each time you make your selection you must justify the choice and ensure it helps answer your research question.

There are two main **types of content analysis**; these are conceptual analysis and relational analysis.

In a conceptual analysis you are looking for a concept and counting how often it appears. It is the simpler and more frequently used type of content analysis and is good for proving a hunch. For example if you felt like a film was mostly about sadness you could code how often the film includes words like 'sad', 'unhappy' or had visuals of people crying, looking upset etc.

In a relational analysis you would go another step here, and would look at how the words or images you have found are used in different settings or combinations to see if it changes the meaning. In our film example this might help us to determine if the director uses certain lighting palettes while sad scenes are played out, or if lighting changes depending on the level of emotion in a scene.

To carry out a content analysis you need to follow these steps;

1. Select the materials (texts) that you will be analyzing.
2. If these are no written texts, then transcribe the text in full.
3. Decide on the type of analysis you will undertake (frequency or concept).
4. Decide how many concepts to code for and how you will distinguish between them.
5. Develop a set of rules for how to code the text, and make sure you write these down to keep your work consistent – they should also appear in your methodology to keep your work transparent.
6. Decide what you will do with irrelevant information.
7. Now read the text, make note of every time a word or idea you are coding appears, either by counting or by highlighting in a set colour to count later.
8. Categorize the results of your coding.
9. Identify if any of those categories can be linked or if there are any emerging themes.
10. If you have more than one text, repeat steps 7-9 with each text.
11. Once all the data is categorized into major or minor categories or themes check it over to ensure there are no mistakes.
12. Now you can begin to see what patterns have emerged, whether categories need to be merged or changed. And you can start to make either qualitative or quantitative analysis of the results shown.

There are lots of **digital tools** available to help with content analysis, and if you are working with a large number of texts it is well worth using them to help with the process. NVivo or Atlas.ti are both very good, and your library will likely have a subscription to one or the other of these. You can also find more information in Carley (1992), Solomon (1993) and Weber (1990). Examples can be found in Roberts (1987) and Adams and Shriebman (1978).

Network analysis

Network Analysis is to help us understand the relationships that occur inside a network and can help us to see where power is held or who influences the shape of the community.

As with all out methods **sampling** is very important. We need to know how much of a network we are going to analyze, but here we also try to collect as much data as possible so we can see the full extent of what is happening. Our main job to ensure we only collect the data related to the network we are studying, but then we need to try and be as complete as possible. This is easier in digital studies, but always important.

The **data** for network analysis can be collected from many different places. Oftentimes we are using digital data from other sources such as Facebook or Twitter in order to make our analyses. It can be difficult or expensive to collect this data due to restrictions by these companies, and the tools for scraping such data can be complex to use. Before undertaking a network analysis project, be sure that you are able to collect the type of data you need, and in a large enough quantity to be able to undertake the work. Here are some suggestions of how to collect digital data:

Blogs – If you are running a blog on the WordPress platform and have admin rights interactions can be downloaded through plugins such as WP All Export – be warned, the data output will need a lot of cleaning to use.

Twitter – Data here can be hard to get hold of, but tools such a TAGS can help you both download and carry out some analysis of tweets: tags.hawksey.info

Other social media – Platforms frequently change their API to make mass downloads harder, but tools such as netlytic.org try to keep up to allow data scrapes from Facebook, Instagram, YouTube, Twitter and RSS feeds.

The analysis of our network normally begins with **creating a visualization** of the network. To do this we need to ensure our data is organized into nodes (people, organizations or events) and edges (their interactions between these). In a simple visualization we can make nodes and edges bigger depending on how many interactions they have. In more complex analysis we can use software tools to run analysis for us to show things like clustering, modularity and centrality, all of which will tell us a great deal of information about the way in which a network operates. None of these things are possible without some software though, and little bit of basic understanding of statistics. One of the simplest tools you can use, and it is free and open source, with plenty of plugins is Gephi, which can be downloaded from gephi.org.

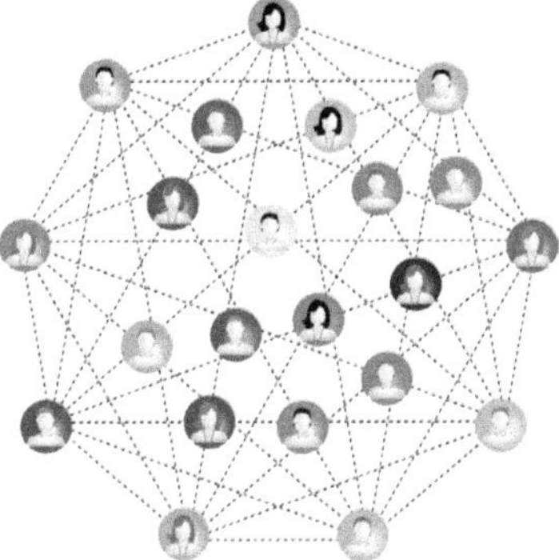

It is beyond the scope of this book to take us through all the types of analysis that you could run on a network, but try downloading some datasets and some software and having a play around – it might inspire a research topic. Just don't let it become procrastination.

Network analysis is becoming ever more popular as a method, as with all methods you need to make sure you are using it because it answers your research question, not just because it is fun. However, its popularity means there are lots of **useful guides** and tools available to help. Try the guide by the Home Office (2016) or Smith et. al. (2009), or take a look at analysis in action in Hu and Racherla (2008) or Schreck and Keim (2013).

This is a really very, very short introduction to research methods, and you should also seek advice from your tutors and other texts to ensure you are doing your research correctly, and following the ethical guidelines of your institution. Doing research for your dissertation is probably one of the most interesting and exciting things you will do during your studies, a real chance for you to get your teeth into the subject in the way that you want to, and to discover something that isn't just interesting to you, but which adds to the body of knowledge about a subject globally. Like we have said though, this chapter has been a very short introduction to some of the skills you will need to help you carry out this research, and you should consider picking up some other books on the subject too in order to ensure you produce the best possible research work.

References

Adams, W., & Shriebman, F. (1978). *Television network news: Issues in content research*. Washington, DC: George Washington University Press.

American Heritage Dictionary (1992). Boston, MA: Houghton Mifflin Harcourt.

Brechin, A., & Siddell, M. (2000). *Using evidence in health and social care*. Sage: London.

Carley, K. (1993). Coding choices for textual analysis: A comparison of content analysis and map analysis. *Sociological Methodology*, 23: 75–126.

Coren, S., & Girgus, J. S. (1978). *Seeing is deceiving: The psychology of visual illusions*. Oxford, UK: Lawrence Erlbaum.

Creswell, J.W. (2013). Steps in conducting a scholarly mixed methods study. Available at https://digitalcommons.unl.edu/cgi/viewcontent.cgi?article=1047&context=dberspeakers

Creswell, J.W., & Clark, V.L.P. (2017). *Designing and conducting mixed methods research*. Thousand Oaks, CA..

Home Office (2016) Social network analysis 'How to Guide'. Home Office. Available from: https://assets.publishing.service.gov.uk/government/uploads/system/uploads/attachment_data/file/491572/socnet_howto.pdf Accessed March 2019.

Hu, C., & Racherla, P. (2008). Visual representation of knowledge networks: A social network analysis of hospitality research domain. *International journal of hospitality management*, 27(2): 302–312.

Kvale S. (1996) Interviews: An introduction to qualitative research interviews. Thousand Oaks, CA: Sage.

Pink, S. (2016). *Digital ethnography,* p. 161. London: Sage.

Murthy, D. (2008). Digital ethnography: An examination of the use of new technologies for social research. *Sociology*, 42(5): 837–855.

Murthy, D. (2011). Emergent digital ethnographic methods for social research. *Handbook of emergent technologies in social research*, pp.158–79. New York: Oxford University Press.

Murthy, D. (2013). Ethnographic Research 2.0: The potentialities of emergent digital technologies for qualitative organizational research. *Journal of Organizational Ethnography*, 2(1): 23–36.

Roberts, S.K. (1987). A content analysis of how male and female protagonists in Newbery Medal and Honor books overcome conflict: Incorporating a locus of control framework. [thesis] Fayetteville, AR: University of Arkansas.

Schreck, T. & Keim, D. (2013). Visual analysis of social media data. *Computer*, *46*(5): 68–75.

Solomon, M. (1993). Content analysis: A potent tool in the searcher's arsenal. *Database*, 16(2): 62–67.

Smith, M.A., Shneiderman, B., Milic-Frayling, N. *et al.* (2009, June). Analyzing (social media) networks with NodeXL. In *Proceedings of the fourth international conference on communities and technologies*, pp. 255–64. ACM.

Weber, R.P. (1990). Basic content analysis, 2nd ed. Newbury Park, CA.

CHAPTER 13

Putting it all together: writing a dissertation

Here we are then, the final chapter. It's all going to come together now. You have learnt to manage your time, you have been a fantastic contributor to your seminars, you've survived group work and submitted your essays. You are a media and communications rock star! But now you need to prove that, once and for all, with the dreaded dissertation! In the last couple of chapters we have looked at some of the additional skills needed, question writing and research skills, but now it is time to bring these together with the skills from the first nine chapters and create something amazing – I mean, even more amazing that what you have done before.

A dissertation usually comes in two halves, a proposal, about what you will do, and a dissertation, about what you did do. This chapter focuses most of its attention on the dissertation, but you can't start a dissertation without a good plan of work, so we will also start by looking at what a good research proposal should look like.

Writing a proposal

A proposal is designed to help you justify and plan your research project, as well as showing how your project contributes to existing research. It is designed to show your lecturer and supervisor that you can conduct research within the time permitted. The main idea though is to help you explore your ideas, and to help you think practically about them. In many ways it is just like an introduction to your thesis, and it is something that will continue to be negotiated as

---

How to cite this book chapter:
Specht, D. 2019. *The Media And Communications Study Skills Student Guide.* Pp. 153–166. London: University of Westminster Press. DOI: https://doi.org/10.16997/book42.m. License: CC-BY-NC-ND 4.0

you progress to the project. So, make it the best you can, but also remember it is just the start of the journey. Also, be aware that there might be differences in requirements depending on your course, so you should be sure to check these before getting started.

TOP TIPS

Avoid anxiety when starting a research project

✓ Establish a writing schedule.

✓ Begin by free writing.

✓ Keep a small notebook with you to write down ideas as you have them.

✓ If it is easier, record yourself speaking about ideas

✓ In a big project, try using different documents on your computer for different sections

✓ Start with more 'clear cut' sections first.

Parts of a proposal

Again, this may differ between courses, so you should check with those who run your degree, but in general a dissertation proposal contains many of the same elements as the dissertation itself. These are (in order);

- A (working) title
- Introduction/background
- Purpose/aims/rationale/research questions
- Review of literature
- Methodology
- Plan of work
- Reference list
- Proposed further reading

While many of these are the same as those in the full dissertation, they will of course be shorter than in the final thesis and your proposal will be in the future tense, because it is your plan. Here is a closer look at each of these parts.

Creating a working title

Your title should tell your readers your research topic and indicate the type of study you will conduct. At the proposal stage, it is a good idea to make your title the same as your research question, this will help you focus all your work and give structure to the proposal. Better still, it will give those reading and marking your proposal an instant idea of what the research is going to be about.

Introduction/background

This is designed to establish the general territory of your work, and to describe the broad foundations of your study. You are now positioning yourself as the expert (yay!) in this field, so you need to provide sufficient background for readers. You should also be introducing the general scope of your project, this will also be in the title, but here you will expand on this much more and explain why you are examining those people or that region and why you have chosen that time-frame. Finally, your introduction should include some really good signposting (see chapter 7) and by this I mean giving an overview of the sections of the dissertation that are to come.

Example of a context paragraph

In a year in which the United States, under Trump, has scrapped their Internet Privacy Law (Lee, 2017), all the while decrying, in an ill-informed manner, wiretapping (MacAskill, 2017),when the UK's Home Secretary, Amber Rudd has called for an equally ill-informed backdoor to WhatsApp (Haynes, 2017), and German parents are told to destroy their children's dolls amid spying fears (Oltermann, 2017), it perhaps seems strange to turn to a book first published in 1964 to help understand the world around us. While it is important to recognize that the world is somewhat different to the 1960s, and that Snowden, in particular, shed a new light on the way in which the war on terror has driven securitization (Lyon, 2015). To really fully understand the modern surveillance state, it is imperative to examine the ongoing conditions of its birth (Jordan, 2015). Huxley, Orwell, and Foucault classically provide the foundation for much of the historical narratives in surveillance studies (Marx, 2016), but the 1960s provided a political climate that would ensure surveillance and privacy would become deeply embedded in our capitalist society and commercial social media platforms (Dwyer, 2016).

*Specht (2017). In-text citations in reference list
at end of chapter.*

Purpose/aims/rationale/research questions

This is part of the introduction and background, but is so important is deserves its own space. Here you explain the goals and research objectives of the study, as well as show the original contributions of your study to the wider research community. Remember, as scary as it might seem, you are now moving towards being the expert in this field. You should also be providing a more detailed account of the points summarized in the introduction, as well as a well-informed rationale for the study. You can also help make your scope very clear by discussing what your study will not address. Here too, it is advised to restate the research question, make it clear and stand out, perhaps on a separate line – this is the most important sentence in the whole proposal/dissertation, make sure it isn't lost. You may also need to define some of the key words or concepts in this section to make is really clear to the reader what you mean, this is especially true of things like 'social media' or 'Web 2.0'.

Focusing on protests against the gold mining company La Colosa in Tolima Department, this article aims to contribute to this field by addressing the questions of (1) whether and how Colombian SMOs use digital and social media in protesting against adverse effects of the mining industry in Colombia, (2) whether these technologies create the critical mass to fight the mining company, and (3) whether they enhance horizontal leadership and knowledge structures. After presenting the contextual background and methodology employed, we address these questions in the 'Results' section. We then discuss the potential of digital and social media in mining protests. The conclusion answers the research questions and discusses the implications.

Specht and Ros-Tonen (2017)

Literature review

Many of your essays will be written a little like a literature review, but your proposal/dissertation will have a very specific part covering this. A literature review is really just focused reading, but the only way for you tutors to know you have done the specific reading is for you to write about it. A literature review is based upon the ideas that other people have already had about the topic you are studying. These ideas are normally presented in books and journal articles, but can also be in films and other resources, and are normally based on research and on primary data or sources. Your job is to give an overview of what has already been published on a topic, but you are doing more than just providing a list of what is available, and you also need to do more than just give a set of summaries; instead you need to use all your skills as a reader, critic and sythensizer that we have learnt though the book thus far, to create a critical analysis of the field. And as American writer and novelist Lisa See reminds us:

Lisa See

The literature review helps you to enlarge your knowledge about the topic, and this is very important, but it also shows you have a number of skills, especially those involving looking for and selecting appropriate reading material. It also shows that you can apply your critical reading, and critical writing skills to the things you have read. The main thing to do in a literature review is to find all the articles related to your topic and then to use summarizing and synthesizing to show your knowledge of these texts and how they fit together as part of the bigger conversation around the topic, highlighting what is, and what isn't, already known about a topic.

You can write your literature review using one of the following approaches:

Chronological approach	Thematic approach
Describe each work or idea in order of when they were written – starting with the earliest available information. ✓ Good for showing how ideas or methodologies have changed over time. ✓ Start by putting your sources/ readings in date order. ✓ Group together ideas and sources from the same time period and examine if there are common themes. ✓ Write about the commonalities and disputes at that time period, and then move to the next one, until you reach the modern day.	*Write about themes or theoretical concepts related to your topic.* ✓ Group your readings by theme, making sure everything is relevant to the topic of your thesis. ✓ Use your skills of synthesis to draw those ideas together, and to highlight disagreements (you need to do more than summarize). ✓ Time might still be important, but isn't the key to the shape of the literature review. ✓ Make new ideas clear to the reader. ✓ Use subheadings to show you are moving to a new topic (but don't use too many).

To help you write the literature review, group different ideas and thoughts together into topics (see chapter 4), and use your skills in summarizing and synthesizing (chapter 8), and your knowledge of paragraph structures (chapter 7) to help you bring those ideas together in a critical way. Finally borrow the linking and connecting words from chapter 10, to join all the paragraphs together. And whatever you do, please, avoid writing 'author one says this, author two says that'. You can though tell the reader where research is lacking, but do be careful to ensure you have done sufficient reading before you claim that an idea is missing.

✗ Do not just write a chronological catalogue of all of the sources – instead evaluate and integrate the previous research together.

✗ Don't be one sided, as all sides of an argument must be clearly explained, to avoid bias and areas of agreement and disagreement should be highlighted.

✗ The literature review should not just be a collection of quotes and paraphrasing from other sources.

Remember, you are entering a scholarly conversation already in progress. The literature review shows that you've been listening and that you have something valuable to say, and to this end you should also keep your language neutral, although you may hedge and use attributive verbs to show your strength of opinion (chapter 9), but you should avoid polemics, praise, and blame.

Knowledge is value-laden and constructed from interests (Hordijk and Baud, 2006: 672); ideas can never be seen as innocent but 'either reinforce or challenge existing social and economic arrangements' (Bryant, 1998: 87). These Foucauldian notions of 'knowledge as power' challenge the much-lauded ability of digital and social media to break down hierarchical structures, create horizontal power and increase political participation through an almost socialist management of knowledge (Castells, 2012; Juris, 2005). There is even 'the risk of furthering inequality if the population of social media users is skewed towards the technologically savvy and those with high human, social, and economic capital' (Valenzuela, 2013: 17). Political ecology has examined the 'politics of knowledge' (Bryant, 1998; Leach and Scoones, 2007; Peet and Watts, 2004) as strategies to construct and politically use multiple knowledges to frame problems and solutions in one's interests – by those in power to justify exclusion of particular groups from access to resources or by those engaged in social action to contest established knowledge and power relations.

Specht and Ros-Tonen (2017). In-text citations in reference list at end of chapter.

Methodology

The methodology means more than just the methods you will use; it is about why you chose those methods and about the details of how you will use them. It should introduce the overall methodological approach and show how this fits the overall research design (Here chapter 12 will be useful). You should also describe the specific methods of data collection and how you intend to analyze and interpret your results (i.e. statistical analysis). One key element often missed by students is making clear the limitations of your research – don't pretend you can do everything. Your time, money and other resources will limit your project, so explain this and give some rationale as to why this is OK.

Everything about your methodology should be explaining why; why is this a good method?; why is it good for your research?; why will you analyze it in that way?; why are those limitations acceptable?; why will your results be significant?; why are you using that sample? Why? Why? Why?! Justify your approach by showing how benefits outweigh potential problems.

It is useful to break down your methodology into subsections. These sections may include selection of participants, interview process, profiles, interpretive and analytic framework, methods of qualitative analysis.

This research analyses journalism-related university curricula in the UK through a mixed methods approach. Firstly, a detailed content analysis was conducted in order to ascertain the extent to which vicarious trauma education features in UK universities. The content description of 63 journalism-related courses from of a total 61 universities were inspected with an examination of the specifications of the courses, the names and descriptions of all modules, coupled with reading specifications and prospects available for potential students… Interviews were used to supplement the content analysis data. Conducted face-to-face or via the phone, they took a semi-structured approach. A total of seven interviews were undertaken, chosen because of their position either as a someone who develops journalism curricula, or who works with recent graduates.

Specht and Tsilman (2018)

Timeline/plan of work

Here you should demonstrate that it is possible to carry out the planned work within the time limits set by the university and to show that you have taking into consideration dates set by the university, the time it takes to establish interviews or to set up surveys and that you have given yourself sufficient writing up and proof reading time.

References and proposed reading

You should of course include a reference list of all the texts cited in the proposals, and these should follow the referencing style of your institution. Following this, you should provide a list of texts that you haven't yet read, but which you plan to. This will help your supervisor see that your reading is heading in the right direction and they will be able to not only see how prepared you are, but will also be able to help guide you in the right direction. This list too should be in the formal style of your institutions referencing guide (See chapter 4).

Remember, a proposal is always just a working document, they are often graded so you need to make them the best they can be, but you will also change and adapt your project as you progress through your studies. You should consider them to be the beginning of the conversation with your supervisor, and something that will be continually negotiated as you progress through your full dissertation.

*   *   *

The dissertation

Now let's look at the dissertation more closely. For this project you will normally be working one-to-one with your supervisor, but it is you who will drive it forwards, and it will bring together all the skills in this book. The dissertation contains all the same things as a proposal, plus a few more, and is much more detailed about what you have been researching. Let's start by looking at the structure of a dissertation. At the start, it has a title page, acknowledgements, contents pages, lists of tables, and an abstract. At the end it will have appendices, references and a glossary. But we will deal with these later, they are the fancy bits – let's start with the main parts of the project. See figure 13.1 for an overview.

We have looked at the parts from introduction to methodology in the proposal section. In your dissertation you will expand on these significantly, but the gist of them is the same – of course now your methodology is in the past tense, about what you *have* done, rather than what you plan to do. For the full dissertation we need to add the following:

Results and discussion

The way that you display your results will depend a lot on how you collected your data. If you have carried out mostly quantitative work then you will need to use charts and tables to show what you have found, and beyond this you should employ some statistical analysis to show if your results are truly significant or not (eek, that's the hard maths… but it is the stuff that will get you the highest grades). If you have done qualitative research, then you might find that your results and discussion are written together as one section where you extract thoughts from interviews or other methods to support your ideas. The important thing though is that however you display your results, your discussion must go beyond describing them. Instead it should analyze them. Use the analytical reading and writing skills from earlier chapters to question your own results in relation to the literature from your literature review. You might like to think about your discussion section as a kind of advanced compare and contrast essay,

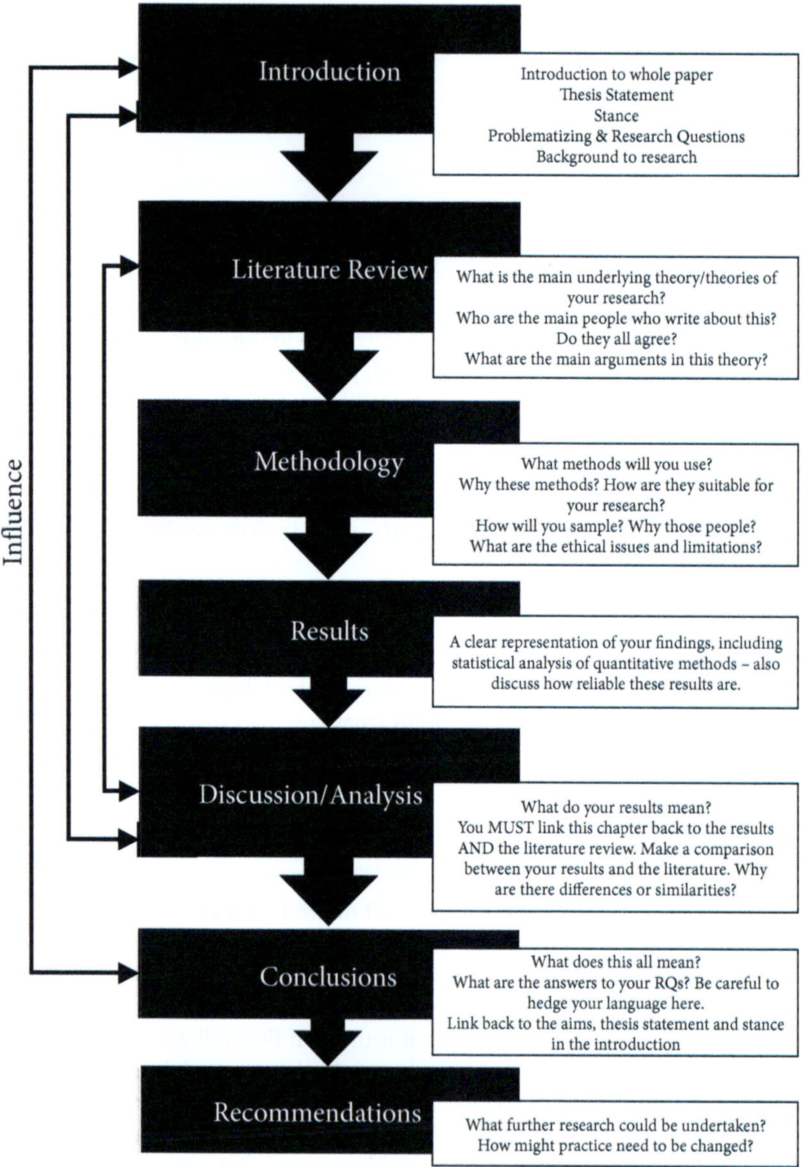

Figure 13.1: Essay template.

where you compare your results with what the literature suggested you would find. Remember though, you must address every research question (and sub question) and every hypothesis (if you have those) as you write your discussion.

Conclusion

The conclusion for your whole dissertation isn't much different to any other conclusion. You must make sure that you answer fully the main question of the thesis, making that really, really clear. Perhaps write something like 'This dissertation set out to ask ________'. Your readers don't want to have to go hunting for the final answer, and there are normally lots of marks for having a strong conclusion, so make it super clear (if yours is the 20th paper your tutor has marked, they might be too tired to see a hidden answer). Remember too to ensure you include nothing new in the conclusion; everything should be a reflection on the work you have done in the pages (so many pages) beforehand.

The trimmings

Now you have the main bread and butter sorted, and wasn't that easy, you can now add the nice bits. Let's have a look at these, starting at the beginning:

Title page
Every university has pretty strict rules about what should be on the title page, and you should check with your institution to ensure you know what these are. It is really important to make a good first impression with the title page, so make sure you get this right.

Acknowledgements
You should include a page where you thank those who have supported your work. This might be family, friends or other people. You should always include your supervisor and other staff who have helped along the way, and also any institutions that have provided you with financial help during your studies.

Contents page
This is pretty self-explanatory, it should be a list of all the subsections of your dissertation along with their page numbers. You should add this last, and also take advantage of the tools included in packages like Word to make this easy.

List tables and illustrations
This, much like the contents page, should be done last, and with the aid of tools built into packages such as Word. It should be a list of all pictures, tables and charts in the dissertation along with their page numbers.

Abstract

This is a brief outline of your work, including what you are studying, how you are studying, and what the results were. Unlike a book blurb, an abstract gives away the ending and findings too. Someone reading your abstract should know everything about your work before they even get to the introductions.

And then at the end comes:

Appendices

Here you can include any supplementary materials from your research. This might include a copy of a survey, interview guides, or transcripts of interviews. Only include things that have been referred to in the main text. And don't put diagrams here that are better suited to being near their descriptions!

References

Don't forget you need to list all the sources you have cited, and you should do so using the preferred referencing methods. See chapter 4 for more on this.

Glossary

You may need to add a glossary of terms to your paper, particularly if it contains a great deal of specialist language or language that has contentious meanings. This might also appear near the front of the paper, just before the introduction.

*   *   *

Well done! You have reached the end! Your dissertation is beautifully bound, set in all the right fonts and line spacing and you have submitted it. It isn't until you look back after submission that you will fully realize how much you have achieved and how much you have progressed and changed. Submitting your work can sometimes leave a bit of an empty feeling, and once the initial celebration has passed you might be wondering where to go next, or if it was all worth it. I'm sure it was, but take one last look at the reflection chapter (6), and remind yourself why you started this process, and consider what were the highs and the lows. This final reflection process will help you take everything you have done forward to the next stages of your life. Good luck!

References

Atzmanstorfer, K., Resl, R., Eitzinger, A., & Izurieta, X. (2014). The GeoCitizen-approach: community-based spatial planning–an Ecuadorian case study. *Cartography and geographic information science, 41*(3), 248–259.

Bryant R (1998). Power, knowledge and political ecology in the third world. *Progress in physical geography* 22: 79–94.

Castells M (2012). *Networks of outrage and hope: Social movements in the internet age.* Cambridge: Polity Press.

Dwyer, T. (2016). *Convergent media and privacy.* Basingstoke and New York: Palgrave Macmillan

Haynes, J. (2017). Backdoor access to WhatsApp? Rudd's call suggests a hazy grasp of encryption. Guardian, [online] Available from: https://www.theguardian.com/technology/2017/mar/27/amber-rudd-call-backdoor-access-hazy-grasp-encryption [Accessed April, 2017]

Hordijk, M. & Baud, I. (2006). The role of research and knowledge generation in collective action and urban governance: How can researchers act as catalysts? *Habitat international* 30: 668–689.

Jordan, T. (2015). *Information politics: Liberation and exploitation in the digital society.* London: Pluto

Juris, J.S. (2005). The new digital media and activist networking within anti-corporate globalization movements. *The annals of the American Academy of Political and Social Science* 597(1): 189–208.

Leach, M. & Scoones, I. (2007). Mobilising Citizens: Social movements and the politics of knowledge (IDS working paper 276). Brighton: IDS.

Lee, D. (2017). Anger as US internet privacy law scrapped. BBC News, [Online] Available from: http://www.bbc.co.uk/news/technology-39427026 [Accessed May 2017].

Lyon, D. (2015). *Surveillance after Snowden.* Malden: Polity.

MacAskill, E. (2017). Trump's Wiretap Paranoia and the Reality of Modern Surveillance. *The Guardian,* [Online] Available from: https://www.theguardian.com/world/2017/mar/06/trumps-wiretap-paranoia-reality-modern-surveillance [Accessed March 2017].

Marx, G.T. (2016). *Windows into the soul: Surveillance and society in an age of high technology.* Chicago: University of Chicago Press

Oltermann, P. (2017). German Parents told to Destroy Doll that can Spy on Children In: [Online] Available from: https://www.theguardian.com/world/2017/feb/17/german-parents-told-to-destroy-my-friend-cayla-doll-spy-on-children [Accessed February 2017]

Peet, R. & Watts, M.J. (eds.) (2004). *Liberation ecologies.* 2nd ed (1st ed 1996). London; New York: Routledge.

Specht, D. (2017). Undressing with the lights on: Surveillance and *The Naked Society* in a digital era. *Westminster papers in communication and culture,* *12*(3), 78–90.

Specht, D. (2018). Neogeography, development and human rights in Latin America. In: *Natural resource development and human rights in Latin America: State and non-state actors in the promotion and opposition to extractivism activities.* School of Advanced Study, London.

Specht, D. & Ros-Tonen, M.A. (2017). Gold, power, protest: Digital and social media and protests against large-scale mining projects in Colombia. *New media and society, 19*(12), 1907–1926.

Specht, D. & Tsilman, J. (2018). Teaching vicarious trauma in the journalism classroom: An examination of educational provision in UK universities. *Journal of applied journalism and media studies, 7*(2), 407–427.

CHAPTER 14

Coda: key skills for media work

As we learnt in the introduction, the key skills in media and communications are being able to write, and being able to handle huge workloads within tight schedules. These two skills enable you to have the space to work on all the exiting editing, designing, discussion, and creative activities through your studies, and all this together will make you a fantastic media and communications practitioner and a critical thinker. This book was designed to help you along the way with those two major parts of your studies, a resource to dip back into as you progress. I hope it has been useful to you, and I hope it will keep you company as you move from your studies to the workplace, where the pressure for you to keep to deadlines, write well and think critically, will be even greater than they are now. It is you though, who will decide whether you will get the most out of your degree, and then use your skills to improve the media and communications landscape in a way that makes the world a little more pleasant for everyone.

> Get a comfortable seat. Good lighting. Identify that time when you are at your most productive and stick to it. Read and stop. Take a break. Drink a lot of water. And always remember to answer the question.
>
> Alfonse – MA Media and Development

As you study, keep an open mind to ideas, keep a positive attitude to criticism. Know that these will be some of the most complex, challenging and thought-provoking months of your life. You will be pushed to work hard, pushed to think hard, pushed to think differently. But these will also be some of the most enjoyable and enlightening months of your life. And as you leave

---

How to cite this book chapter:

Specht, D. 2019. *The Media And Communications Study Skills Student Guide.* Pp. 167–168. London: University of Westminster Press. DOI: https://doi.org/10.16997/book42.n. License: CC-BY-NC-ND 4.0

the university, take these skills with you, keep that open mind, keep that critical edge, as you look back on your studies, you will surely see how much you have changed and grown as a person.

Good luck with all your studies, and in all your future work and endeavours!

Doug

About the Author

Doug Specht (SFHEA) is Director of Teaching and Learning, School of Media and Communications at the University of Westminster. He has taught for fifteen years across a range of sectors and countries. He now teaches primarily on digital media and communications at both undergraduate and postgraduate level. His teaching also includes teaching study skills across the School of Media and Communications and the School of Arts. He also works with staff to develop their teaching practice, contributing to MA courses in Higher Education. He holds a PGCE, TESOL, and an MA in Higher Education.

A Chartered Geographer, his research examines how knowledge is constructed and codified through digital and cartographic artifacts, focusing on development issues, and he has written on this subject in numerous books and papers. He has also spoken on topics of data ethics and mapping practices at conferences and invited lectures around the world. He is a member of the editorial board at *Westminster Papers in Communication and Culture*, and sits on BSi committee IST/36 Geographic Information, where he focuses on geographic data in the Sustainable Development Goals (SDGs). He is the editor of the forthcoming book *Mapping Crisis*, and co-editor of the forthcoming book project *The Routledge Handbook of Geospatial Technology and Society* with Alexander Kent.

Acknowledgments

This book has been made possible by all the teachers and students I have worked with since I began working in education. Your ideas, support, tips and advice have been invaluable in both my own teaching, and in the writing of this book, and I thank you for your generosity in sharing them. Thank you also to those who have worked with me to make this book possible. A special thanks to Andrew Lockett who has worked tirelessly to help bring my vision for this book to life. (*Doug Specht*).

Cover image graphics and several images, ©Shutterstock. The author and publisher have made every effort to identify and contact copyright holders for images where requested under creative commons or other licenses. Third party text material is used in accordance with exceptions for educational use, criticism and review and fair dealing with acknowledgments accordingly provided in the text close to use with the following exceptions hereby noted and gratefully acknowledged: p36; 'Linear Notes' image: www.mindmeister.com; 'Spider Notes' image; www.pinterest.co.uk/pin/185210603412882868. Should any omission or error have occurred in relation to text or images these will be corrected if notification is made to the publisher.

Quote sources used as follows: p.7 (Luxemburg, R, 2004, The *Rosa Luxemburg reader*. NYU Press and Orwell, G. 2014. *Why I write*. Penguin); p.15 (Widely attributed to Achebe, for example by thesparklewritershub.com); p.16 (From essay 'Work and Pleasure', in Adorno, T., 2002. *Adorno: The stars down to earth and other essays on the irrational in culture.* Routledge); p.22 (Tannen, D. cited in Berson, A. S. and Stieglitz, R. G., 2013. *Leadership conversations: Challenging high potential managers to become great leaders.* John Wiley & Sons); p.26 (Thoreau, H. D., 2013. *Delphi complete works of Henry David Thoreau.* Delphi Classics); p.27 (Poe, E. A. , 1849, *The works of Edgar Allan Poe,* Volume 3. Widdleton); p.32 (Marshall McLuhan, *The best of ideas,* CBC Radio, 1967); p.52 (Twain, M. cited in Halbert, D., 2016. *Advocacy and public speaking.* University of Chester Press); p.57 (Carneige, D. Cited in Crux, H. E., 2016. *Public speaking, simplified and demystified: Communication basics to create lasting impressions!* Lulu.com); p.58 (Widely attributed to Arendt, for example by brainyquote. com); p.62 (Widely attributed to Gibbon, for example by goodreads.com); p.79 (Butler, O. E. *cited in* Chamberlain, L., 2018. *Inspiring writing in primary schools.* Learning Matters); p.90 (Du Bois, W. E. B., 1997. *The Correspondence of WEB Du Bois* (Vol. 3). University of Massachusetts Press); p.91 (Foucault, M. 1979/2013, *Archaeology of knowledge.* Routledge); p.92 (Benjamin, W. 1999, *Selected writings. Vol 1.* Belknap/Harvard University Press: Cambridge, MA); p.123 (Wallace, D. F., 2008 Plain old untrendy troubles and emotions. Guardian [Online] Available at: https://www.theguardian.com/books/2008/sep/20/ fiction); p.127 (Jenkins, H., 2006. Eight Traits of the New Media Landscape. [Online] Available at: http://henryjenkins.org/blog/2006/11/eight_traits_of_ the_new_media.html; Hall's thought here is a summary of ideas found in Chen, K. H., & Morley, D. (eds.), 2006, *Stuart Hall: Critical dialogues in cultural studies.* Routledge); p.131 (Walker, A. cited in Hull, G. T., Bell-Scott, P., & Smith, B. 1982. *All the women are white, all the blacks are men, but some of us are brave: Black women's studies.* Feminist Press); p.135 (In Gadotti, M. 1994, *Reading Paulo Freire: His life and work.* SUNY Press); p.157 (See, L., 2009, *Snow Flower and the secret fan: A novel.* Random House).

Weekly work planner and other supplementary template files available at: DOI: https://doi.org/10.16997/book42.1

Index

Printed and bound by CPI Group (UK) Ltd, Croydon, CR0 4YY

07/07/2026

14916228-0004